"It is hard to imagine a better introducti[o] for pastors, seminary students, or general the most respected Old Testament scholars of our time, makes a compelling case for the relevance of the psalms for both public and private worship. *The Psalter Reclaimed* is engagingly written, well informed, practical, and genuinely inspiring."

> **Gordon P. Hugenberger,** Senior Minister, Park Street Church, Boston; Adjunct Professor of Old Testament, Gordon-Conwell Theological Seminary

"I am grateful to Professor Wenham for gathering in one volume many of his special studies on the Psalms, for many the favorite book of the First Testament. The essays included here not only introduce readers to the history of scholarship on the Psalter, but also provide us with hermeneutical guidelines for interpreting the book. And best of all, they make accessible to us its inspiring and transforming message."

> **Daniel I. Block,** Gunther H. Knoedler Professor of Old Testament, Wheaton College

"This collection of essays is vintage Gordon Wenham. Taking seriously both the church's tradition of using the psalms and the possibilities provided by the latest exegesis, he shows us what it means to make use of the Psalter and how this can be done. The result is a rich theological and exegetical brew that nourishes both heart and head."

> **David G. Firth,** Lecturer in Old Testament, St John's College, Nottingham, United Kingdom; author, *Hear, O Lord: A Spirituality of the Psalms*

"This book's many virtues make it instructive and refreshing: I appreciate its stress on the psalms' place in public worship, and the speech-act notion of self-involvement in singing. Wenham also offers helpful arguments for respecting the titles of the psalms. And the creative approach to 'canonical reading' allows us to view each psalm both as a composition for public singing and as a part of the canonical book (which may guide our interpretation). I heartily commend this work!"

> **C. John Collins,** Professor of Old Testament, Covenant Theological Seminary

"As someone who comes from an Asian (Filipino) context, I find it heartwarming to read *The Psalter Reclaimed*. This book helps those of us in the majority world, where the church continues to grow, by showing us a way of reading the psalms that brings us closer to God."

Federico G. Villanueva, Associate Professor and Director of Biblical Studies, Alliance Graduate School, Manila, Philippines; author, *It's OK to Be Not OK: The Message of the Lament Psalms*

"*The Psalter Reclaimed* is an absolute delight! This study takes us on a whirlwind journey through the book of Psalms, hitting all the high points along the way. Themes like the dynamic of singing our theology; reading the Psalms as a book, as prayers, and in the light of Christ; and dealing with the 'nasty' psalms are all considered with real exegetical insight and winsomeness. If your desire is to 'reclaim the Psalter,' then this is definitely the book for you."

Jamie A. Grant, Lecturer in Biblical Studies, Highland Theological College, Dingwall, Scotland; author, *The King as Exemplar: The Function of Deuteronomy's Kingship Law in the Shaping of the Book of Psalms*

The PSALTER RECLAIMED

The

PSALTER
RECLAIMED

Praying and Praising with the Psalms

Gordon
Wenham

WHEATON, ILLINOIS

The Psalter Reclaimed: Praying and Praising with the Psalms
Copyright © 2013 by Gordon J. Wenham

Published by Crossway
      1300 Crescent Street
      Wheaton, Illinois 60187

Cover design: Studio Gearbox

First printing 2013
Printed in the United States of America

Trade paperback ISBN: 978-1-4335-3396-9
Mobipocket ISBN: 978-1-4335-3398-3
PDF ISBN: 978-1-4335-3397-6
ePub ISBN: 978-1-4335-3399-0

Library of Congress Cataloging-in-Publication Data

Wenham, Gordon J.
   The Psalter reclaimed : praying and praising with the
Psalms / Gordon Wenham.
     p. cm.
   Includes bibliographical references and index.
   ISBN 978-1-4335-3396-9
   1. Bible. O.T. Psalms—Criticism, interpretation, etc.
I. Title.
BS1430.52.W465   2013
223'.206—dc23   2012028651

Crossway is a publishing ministry of Good News Publishers.

VP			22	21	20	19	18	17	16	15	14	13
15	14	13	12	11	10	9	8	7	6	5	4	3	2	1

Contents

Acknowledgments   9

Abbreviations   11

1   What Are We Doing Singing the Psalms?   13

2   Praying the Psalms   37

3   Reading the Psalms Canonically   57

4   Reading the Psalms Messianically   81

5   The Ethics of the Psalms   103

6   The Imprecatory Psalms   129

7   Psalm 103: The Song of Steadfast Love   147

8   The Nations in the Psalms   161

Works Cited   187

General Index   193

Index of Scripture   197

Acknowledgments

This collection contains various lectures on the Psalms that I gave between 1997 and 2010. Their publication started with a request to publish the four (chaps. 2–5) that I gave at The Southern Baptist Theological Seminary in 2006, two of which have already been published elsewhere. They are republished here with permission, as indicated at their respective chapters. I have added some others to this core to round out the collection. This means that while the lectures and essays have been slightly adapted to this book form, there is inevitably some overlap between them.

Concurrently with giving these lectures I was working on a book on the ethics of the Psalms, recently published as *Psalms as Torah* (Grand Rapids: Baker Academic, 2012), which particularly develops ideas first explored in the essay "The Ethics of the Psalms."

Abbreviations

BZAW	Beihefte zur Zeitschrift für die alttestamentliche Wissenschaft
ESV	English Standard Version
KJV	King James Version
NIDOTTE	*New International Dictionary of Old Testament Theology and Exegesis.* Edited by Willem A. VanGemeren. 5 vols., Carlisle: Paternoster, 1997
NIV	New International Version
NLT	New Living Translation
NPNF[1]	*Nicene and Post-Nicene Fathers*, Series 1
NRSV	New Revised Standard Version
RSV	Revised Standard Version
TDOT	*Theological Dictionary of the Old Testament.* Edited by G. J. Botterweck and H. Ringgren. 15 vols. Grand Rapids: Eerdmans, 1974–2004
THWAT	*Theologisches Handwörterbuch zum Alten Testament.* Edited by Ernst Jenni and Claus Westermann. 2 vols. Munich: Kaiser Verlag, 1971–1976

CHAPTER 1

What Are We Doing Singing the Psalms?[1]

"Let me write the songs of a nation, and I care not who writes its laws." So said the distinguished Scottish politician Andrew Fletcher in a book published in 1704. Fletcher was a forerunner of the Scottish National Party in fighting for Scottish independence. His comment is the more intriguing in that as a member of the Scottish parliament he was very active in promoting legislation. Yet he recognized the power of song to capture and mold people's imaginations and attitudes to life.

This insight, though, seems to have eluded most biblical scholars. The significance of the Psalms for biblical ethics has been surprisingly overlooked. Their unique character as powerful shapers of individual virtues and social attitudes is largely ignored in books on Old Testament ethics. It is my belief that reciting the psalms, and specially singing them, has profoundly influenced both Jewish and Christian theology and ethics.

Most, if not all, of the psalms were originally composed to be sung in temple worship, and through the centuries they have continued to be sung in church and synagogue. So in this chapter I first want to give a brief overview of the history of their liturgical use and discuss the peculiar impact of setting their words to music. But the Psalter's present arrangement suggests that when the psalms were collected together as a book, it may well be that a secondary use for them developed, namely, as a resource for private meditation and devotion. I want to suggest that the Psalter is

---

[1] Originally delivered at Highland Theological College, Dingwall, Scotland, October 24, 2008; first published in *Irish Biblical Studies* 28 (2010): 147–69. Used by permission.

a deliberately organized anthology designed for memorization. In the days before the printing press Scripture was regularly memorized, and certain features of the Psalter suggest that it was used this way. I shall reflect on the implications that memorization has for their authority.

Finally I want to use speech-act theory to explore what we are doing when we recite publicly or sing the psalms. I will suggest that in some ways singing a psalm or hymn is like taking an oath: we are committing ourselves in a binding way to a particular set of beliefs and embracing a lifestyle. Perhaps this is not evident on the surface, but I hope to show that there is much more to singing the psalms than exercising our lungs!

Singing the Psalms down the Ages

The books of Chronicles contain many references to psalm singing, both in the temple and outside it. They tell how David appointed the Levites to lead worship. Some of the Levites carried the ark to Jerusalem while others sang and played musical instruments (1 Chron. 15:15–16). When the Israelites arrived in Jerusalem, Chronicles records that David appointed the Levites to sing thanksgivings. First Chronicles 16:8–36 gives the texts sung on this occasion. These correspond to Psalm 105:1–15 (1 Chron. 16:8–22); Psalm 96:1–13 (1 Chron. 16:23–34); and Psalm 106:47–48 (1 Chron. 16:35–36). Presumably these are to be understood as just a selection of the psalms used on this great occasion. It is not clear what others could have been used.[2]

The use of psalms in temple worship is confirmed by a study of the psalms themselves. Conventional form criticism has ignored the titles of psalms and developed its theories on the basis of the content of the psalms alone. The numerous references to entering the temple and offering sacrifice, and the obvious relevance of many psalms to the great national festivals, such as Passover and Tabernacles, led

---

[2] It is noteworthy that none of these psalms has a title in the Psalter, let alone is called a psalm of David. It may be that Chronicles understands the title "Of David" in Psalm 103 to apply to the following untitled psalms (104–6).

scholars such as Gunkel and Mowinckel to argue that many of the psalms were composed for use in the pre-exilic temple.

The titles of the psalms point in the same direction. One says it is "for the thank offering" (Psalm 100, RSV), another "for the Sabbath" (92). Many others have the heading "To the choirmaster," if that is the right translation, while sometimes the tune seems to be specified "according to Lilies" (45, 69, 80) or "according to the Dove on Far-off Terebinths" (56). The book of Nehemiah tells of two choirs processing around the just-rebuilt walls of Jerusalem singing psalms (Neh. 12:31–43).

Among the Dead Sea Scrolls, manuscripts of the Psalms are more frequent than any other type, attesting their widespread use among Jews in New Testament times. The Gospels describe Jesus's triumphal entry into Jerusalem and the crowds' greeting him with Psalm 118, "Hosanna! Blessed is he who comes in the name of the Lord!" (Mark 11:9; cf. Ps. 118:25–26). Jesus himself and his disciples sang this psalm and the immediately preceding ones at the Last Supper.[3] The early church continued the practice of singing the psalms. Paul assumed that the Corinthians, Colossians, and Ephesians sang the psalms: "Let the word of Christ dwell in you richly, teaching and admonishing one another in all wisdom, singing psalms and hymns and spiritual songs, with thankfulness in your hearts to God" (Col. 3:16; cf. 1 Cor. 14:26; Eph. 5:19).

By the beginning of "the fourth century the memorization of the Psalms by many Christians and their habitual use as songs in worship by all Christians about whom we know were matters of long-standing tradition."[4] The use of the Psalms in private prayer and public worship is most eloquently advocated by Athanasius in his letter to Marcellinus. He wrote:

> Whatever your particular need or trouble, from this same book you can select a form of words to fit it, so that you not merely hear and then pass on, but learn the way to remedy your ill.[5]

---

[3] The hymn they sang is the Great Hallel, Psalms 113–18, used at Passover and other festivals.

[4] William L. Holladay, *The Psalms through Three Thousand Years* (Minneapolis: Fortress, 1993), 165.

[5] Athanasius, *On the Incarnation*, with appendix "On the Interpretation of the Psalms," ed. and trans. a religious of C.S.M.V. (New York: St Vladimir's Seminary Press, 1977), 103.

If you want to declare anyone to be blessed; you find the way to do it in Psalm 1, and likewise in 32, 41, 112, 119, and 128. If you want to rebuke the conspiracy of the Jews against the Saviour, you have Psalm 2. If you are persecuted by your own family and opposed by many, say Psalm 3; and when you would give thanks to God at your affliction's end, sing 4 and 75 and 116. When you see the wicked wanting to ensnare you and you wish your prayer to reach God's ears, then wake up early and sing 5.[6]

Athanasius sees Psalm 32 as particularly appropriate at baptisms: "Whenever a number of you want to sing together, being all good and upright men, then use the 33rd ["Shout for joy in the LORD, O you righteous! / Praise befits the upright]."[7]

When St. Benedict established monasteries in the sixth century, he prescribed that psalms should be used at the eight services of the day. Some psalms (e.g., 51, 134) were used every day, and in the course of the whole week all the psalms would be sung. But it was not just in the monasteries that the psalms were used. In the Middle Ages the Psalter was the only part of the Bible a layman was likely to own. It is said that King Alfred the Great "was frequent in psalm-singing and prayer at the hours both of the day and night."[8] Martin Luther, as a good monk, was brought up on the Psalms, and Luther scholars think that it was his study of the Psalms that led him to his understanding of justification by faith.

Certainly Luther encouraged the singing of the psalms in public worship. He said, "The whole Psalter, Psalm by Psalm, should remain in use, and the entire Scripture, lesson by lesson, should continue to be read to the people."[9] His first hymnbook contained twenty-three hymns, of which six were versions of psalms. The Reformed tradition was even more diligent in producing singable metrical versions of the psalms. Bucer, Calvin, Hopkins, and

---

[6] Ibid., 107–8.
[7] Ibid., 109.
[8] John A. Giles, *Six Old English Chronicles* (London: Bell & Dadly, 1872), 68, quoted in Holladay, *The Psalms through Three Thousand Years*, 177.
[9] Timothy E. Lull, ed., *Luther's Basic Theological Writings*, 468, quoted in Holladay, *The Psalms through Three Thousand Years*, 195.

Tate and Brady produced collections of metrical psalms. These continue in use in many Presbyterian churches even today. In other churches the situation is mixed. Since Vatican II, Roman Catholics have been singing more of the psalms, but I fear that in many Protestant churches the psalms have been displaced by hymns and songs. Indeed in a seminary at which I was examiner I was shocked to find there was no study of the Psalms in their BD (MDiv) program!

But what makes singing so significant? Singing, as opposed to mere recitation, helps concentration. Athanasius expressed it well: "For to sing the Psalms demands such concentration of a man's whole being on them that, in doing it, his usual disharmony of mind and corresponding bodily confusion is resolved, just as the notes of several flutes are brought by harmony to one effect."[10]

Luther made much the same point: adding music to the words involves the whole personality in the act of worship.

> Music is to be praised as second only to the Word of God because by her are all the emotions swayed. Nothing on earth is more mighty to make the sad gay and the gay sad, to hearten the downcast, mellow the overweening, temper the exuberant, or mollify the vengeful. . . . That is why there are so many songs and psalms. This precious gift has been bestowed on men alone to remind them that they are created to praise and magnify the Lord.[11]

David Ford, Regius Professor of Theology at Cambridge, more recently commented:

> What does [singing] do with the crucial Christian medium of words? It does with them what praise aims to do with the whole of reality: it takes them up into a transformed, heightened expression, yet without at all taking away their ordinary meaning. Language itself is transcended and its delights and power

---

[10] Athanasius, *On the Incarnation*, 114.
[11] Roland H. Bainton, *Here I Stand: A Life of Martin Luther* (New York: Mentor, 1955), 268–69.

are intensified, and at the same time those who join in are bound together more strongly. So singing is a model of the way praise can take up ordinary life and transpose it to a higher level without losing what is good in other levels.[12]

So perhaps Andrew Fletcher was right to suggest that composing a nation's songs is even more significant than drafting its laws.

Singing the psalms also helps us memorize them. I am afraid Anglican chants rarely do this for me, but some of Handel's settings in the Messiah and his Chandos anthems stick in my memory, as of course do hymns based on psalms such as "As Pants the Hart for Cooling Streams," (Psalm 42), "Jesus Shall Reign Where'er the Sun" (Psalm 72), and "Praise My Soul the King of Heaven" (Psalm 103). But whether or not the psalms were set to music, people in olden days were very good at memorization. As I was writing this, I came across a comment in *The Times*[13] that the Romans "were commonly able to recite the *Aeneid*, a 10,000-line poem, word for word; generals would know the name of every soldier in their armies; orators would deliver three-hour speeches without notes."

The same was true among the Greeks. At their dinner parties Greek men were expected to show off their learning by reciting the poems of Homer. They were also performed at great festivals, such as the Panhellenic games at Olympia and Nemea. The Homeric corpus is about as long as the whole Old Testament, so reciting portions of it represents quite a feat of memory by these Greek scribes. In his book *Writing on the Tablet of the Heart*, David M. Carr has argued that similar practices were common among the neighbors of ancient Israel: the Babylonians, Egyptians, and the Canaanites of Ugarit. It is therefore highly probable that the Israelites did the same. Scribes, maybe drawn from the Levites, would have memorized books of the Bible and proclaimed them at the great festivals. It is possible that they also went round the villages giving recitations of them.

---

[12] David F. Ford and Daniel W. Hardy, *Living in Praise: Worshipping and Knowing God* (London: Darton, Longman and Todd, 2005), 19.

[13] *The Times*, October 9, 2008, sec. 2, p. 5.

However, what would the ordinary Israelite have had in the way of Scripture? Certainly not a copy of the Old Testament. Books were prohibitively expensive before the days of printing. Of course the Israelites might have remembered bits of what the scribes recited, especially if they attended the national festivals regularly. But is there a part of the Bible that ordinary people might have memorized themselves? If any book might qualify, it is the Psalter.

Various features make the Psalter, in Luther's words, a mini-Bible. It gives an overview of history from creation through to the conquest of Canaan (e.g., Psalms 104–6). Many psalm titles relate to episodes in David's life. Some clearly celebrate worship in the Jerusalem temple. Other psalms relate the sacking of Jerusalem and reflect on the experience of exile. Thus those who sing the psalms will be constantly reminded of the character of God, his dealings with Israel, and the sin of man. More than that, they will be taught many principles of ethics. Not only are many laws alluded to and underlined, but the Psalter itself is presented as a new Pentateuch arranged in five books like Genesis to Deuteronomy, which the worshipper is encouraged to mutter[14] to himself day and night (Ps. 1:2). That he can do this as well by night as by day indicates that he has learned them by heart: he is most unlikely to be reading a scroll by candlelight. Above all, the Psalter provides the reciter or singer of them with prayers that suit every mood. As Calvin put it:

> I am in the habit of calling this book . . . "The Anatomy of all the parts of the soul," for not an affection will any one find in himself, an image of which is not reflected in this mirror. Nay, all the griefs, sorrows, fears, misgivings, hopes, cares, anxieties; in short, all the disquieting emotions with which the minds of men are wont to be agitated, the Holy Spirit hath here pictured.[15]

Not only does the content make the Psalter useful as a

---

[14] Hebrew *hagah* is often translated "meditate," which Westerners would understand as silent thought. But other passages use this term of pigeons cooing or lions growling (Isa. 31:4; 38:14), so speaking aloud is envisaged when humans "meditate."

[15] John Calvin, *A Commentary on the Psalms of David* (Oxford: Tegg, 1840), 1:vi.

summary of the Old Testament and its teaching, but there are many features that may be viewed as aids to memory. Most obvious are the acrostic psalms: working through the alphabet verse by verse would certainly assist memorization. Then there are the verbal linkages between one psalm and the next, grouping of similar themed psalms, and the use of parallelism, alliteration, assonance, chiasms, and rhyme. All these could help the psalms be memorized. Delitzsch and Alexander are two nineteenth-century commentators who draw attention to some of these features. In recent times the commentaries of Hossfeld and Zenger in German and Vesco in French have provided a more exhaustive account of these features. Given the memorization techniques of the ancients, it is possible that they would not have needed these clues to help them. Nevertheless these clues do make modern readers of the Psalms ask questions about the potential for memorization.

But does history provide parallels to a book being produced for lay as opposed to specialist reciters, and is not the Psalter too long a work for ordinary people to learn by heart? In Greece there were abridged versions of the classics that could be memorized, even though such productions were looked down on by the purists. In India anthologies of Buddhist scriptures (c. AD 100 and 700) were produced with the aim of mass learning. But the most interesting parallels come from the church in North Africa in the third and fifth centuries.

In the course of their catechetical instruction new converts were expected to learn a collection of Bible verses. Cyprian's *Three Books of Testimonies for Quirinus* "is about 33,000 words long . . . and contains rather more than 700 excerpts" and "would take about three and a half hours to read aloud."[16] Augustine's *Mirror of Sacred Scripture*

> is roughly 60,000 words long. . . . It would take something over six hours to read aloud at a speed of 160 words per minute. It

---

[16] Paul J. Griffiths, *Religious Reading: The Place of Reading in the Practice of Religion* (New York: Oxford University Press, 1999), 165.

contains a little over 800 excerpts, of very varied lengths. The longest is seven pages . . . , containing almost all of Matthew 5–7; there are a number of very short excerpts . . . ; and there is everything in between. The mean length of an excerpt is about seventy words, but there are few of just that length. Augustine, much more than Cyprian, is happy to give lengthy excerpts interspersed with very brief ones. There is no standard length for an excerpt.[17]

As modern Westerners we are astonished that new converts could be asked to learn so much, but it must have seemed an easy task compared with learning all the works of Homer or even the *Aeneid.* We can see how Cyprian and Augustine worked in excerpting the Bible. Cyprian arranged his texts topically, whereas Augustine just kept the extracts in the biblical order. Paul Griffiths observes similar features in the Buddhist anthologies. One contains six thousand verses and "almost all of it consists of excerpts from other works." The editor contributed at most 5 percent of the text, mostly "very brief phrases introducing an excerpt and giving the title of the work from which it was taken."[18] There are about 312 excerpts, varying in length from a short sentence to 172 verses.

The Psalter fits this pattern of anthology. The psalms are discrete units, and the variety of titles has long suggested to commentators that they are drawn from a variety of earlier collections, for example, a Davidic Psalter, an Asaphite collection, and so on. The length of the Psalter is comparable to the Buddhist and Christian anthologies that Griffiths cites. The Psalter contains 2,527 verses, which, read at nine verses to the minute,[19] would take about four and a half hours to recite. The variation in length of individual psalms is comparable to other anthologies.

I think this view of the Psalter has much to be said in its favor, but I would not pretend to have offered hard proof. Whether or not

---

[17] Ibid., 169.

[18] Ibid., 133.

[19] This is the speed at which Griffiths reckons the Buddhist texts would have been recited. This is quite slow for reading the psalms. Kol Israel ("Voice of Israel" radio) read them unhurriedly at ten verses per minute.

it is an anthology of earlier texts, I believe it extremely probable that it was intended to be memorized. And we need to explore the significance of memorization. Once again Griffiths has some very astute observations. Memorization goes hand in hand with religious reading. This is quite different from modern reading styles. Most modern readers approach texts in what Griffiths terms a consumerist fashion. You read what you like, read when you like, and accept what you like in what you read. Then you discard what you have just read and move on to read something else. In Griffiths's opinion this characterizes our approach to reading everything, from newspaper articles to academic monographs.

The approach of religious readers is quite different. They see the work read as an infinite resource. "It is a treasure-house, an ocean, a mine; the deeper religious readers dig . . . the greater will be their reward."[20] The work read is treated with great reverence. Griffiths explains: "For the religious reader, the work read is an object of overpowering delight and great beauty. It can never be discarded because it can never be exhausted. It can only be reread, with reverence and ecstasy."[21] Psalm 119:97 gives expression to this outlook.

> Oh how I love your law!
>   It is my meditation all the day.

Griffiths continues, "For [religious] readers the ideally read work is the memorized work, and the ideal mode of rereading is by memorial recall." As a reader memorizes a text, he becomes textualized; that is, he embodies the work he has committed to memory. "Ezekiel's eating of the prophetic scroll . . . is a representation of the kind of incorporation and internalization involved in religious reading: the work is ingested, used for nourishment, incorporated: it becomes the basis for rumination and for action."[22]

Further, "A memorized work (like a lover, a friend, a spouse,

---

[20] Griffiths, *Religious Reading*, 41.
[21] Ibid., 42.
[22] Ibid., 46.

a child) has entered into the fabric of its possessor's intellectual and emotional life in a way that makes deep claims upon that life, claims that can only be ignored with effort and deliberation."[23] Medieval theologians used lively images to describe the relationship between the memorized work and the reciter. Bernard of Clairvaux described the Bible as the wine cellar of the Holy Spirit.[24] Anselm of Canterbury compared Scripture to honeycomb: "Taste the goodness of your Redeemer, burn with love for your Saviour. Chew the honeycomb of his words, suck their flavour, which is more pleasing than honey, swallow their health-giving sweetness."[25]

One hopes that this is the experience of many as they sing and pray the psalms. They mold one's character and heighten one's love of God.

The Psalms as Speech Acts

But there is even more to the impact that the Psalms make on their users, as speech-act theorists have pointed out. The didactic function of prayers, hymns, and songs is evident. When we say the Lord's Prayer we are committing ourselves to certain beliefs and attitudes. Its opening invocation, "Our Father, who art in heaven," clearly teaches some very basic theology about the relationship between God and his people. If they should call him Father, then they are his sons. It is a relationship that involves intimacy (he is our Father) and also distance (he is in heaven). But there is also an ethical dimension to calling God our Father in heaven. In a traditional patriarchal culture the father was an authority figure whose word was law in the family: he had to be obeyed. By saying "Our Father" the early church at least was acknowledging divine authority and implicitly submitting to it.

The same is true of hymns. The hymns and songs of apparently liturgy-free churches have much the same role as the prescribed prayers of liturgical worship. Both implicitly and explicitly they

---

[23] Ibid., 47.

[24] Ibid., 42, quoting Bernard's thirty-fifth sermon on the Song of Songs.

[25] Griffiths, 43 quoting Anselm, *Opera Omnia*, ed. F. S. Schmitt (Edinburgh: Thomas Nelson, 1946), 3:84.

teach theology and ethics. Christmas carols, such as "Hark the Herald Angels Sing" or "O Come All Ye Faithful," proclaim and explain aspects of the incarnation. "When I Survey the Wondrous Cross" and "There Is a Green Hill" teach about the meaning of the crucifixion. Graham Kendrick's "Servant King" has the refrain,

This is our God, the Servant King:
he calls us now to follow him.

George Herbert wrote,

Teach me, my God and king,
in all things thee to see
and what I do in anything
to do it as for thee.

Thus singing hymns inculcates a variety of Christian truths and ethical principles: indeed the worshipper is compelled to subscribe to them in the very act of singing. If one objects and refuses to sing a particular line or verse, it may well be noticed! Thus there is a strong social pressure to conform as well.

The teaching power of hymns is acknowledged in a recent hymnal, titled *Hymns Old and New*. The compilers have rewritten many old hymns to eliminate their alleged sexism or militarism. For instance, "Onward Christian soldiers, marching as to war" becomes "Onward Christian pilgrims, Christ will be our light"! They comment:

We were also concerned that the book should use positive and appropriate images, and decided that militarism and triumphalism were, therefore, not appropriate. We recognise that military imagery is used in the Bible, but history, including current events, shows only too clearly the misuse to which those images are open. All too often in the Christian and other religions, texts advocating spiritual warfare are used to justify the self-serving ambitions behind temporal conflicts. Christian "triumph" is the triumph of love which "is not envious or boastful or arrogant" (1 Corinthians 13:4): the triumph of the cross.[26]

I doubt that many readers will agree with these sentiments, but this attention to what hymns affirm does alert us to what is happening when we pray, and when we sing hymns or psalms. The psalms teach us the fundamentals of the faith and instruct us too in ethics.

But the psalms do even more. Singing them commits us in attitudes, speech, and actions. In the mid-twentieth century, two philosophers, J. L. Austin and J. R. Searle, shed light on the nature of speech. They pointed out that speech is much more than the exchange of information: it changes situations. A promise, for example, lays an obligation on the one who makes the promise and creates an expectation in the one who hears it. This has implications for our use of the Psalms, as we shall see.

The Psalms differ from other parts of the Bible in that they are meant to be recited or sung as prayers. That makes them public address to God. By using them as prayers or singing them, worshippers declare their faith and their commitment to God's ways. But narrative and law are different. The Old Testament narratives were presumably recited by storytellers, but they rarely make explicit their judgments on the actions that are recited, so the moral of the story might have been missed and certainly did not have to be endorsed by the listeners. They could just ignore the point, as I suspect many listening to worthy sermons often do.

The same is true of the laws. Few people would have had written copies of the law. In the light of the practice in neighboring cultures, it would seem likely that most people's knowledge would have come from hearing recitations of the laws at religious festivals. But, once again, for the listener the reception of the law was essentially passive. One listened to the law and maybe an explanation of it by a preacher, and then it was up to the hearer to keep it or reject it as he saw fit (Neh. 8:1–10). As long as he did not publicly reject or break the law, he would be accepted, socially at least.

---

[26] Foreword to *Hymns Old and New: New Anglican Edition* (Bury St Edmunds: Kevin Mayhew, 1996).

Thus receiving the teaching of the law or the history books of the Old Testament was basically a silent, passive affair.

But reciting the psalms is quite different. The one who prays the psalms is taking their words on his lips and saying them to God in a personal and solemn way. An example is Psalm 7:8–9.

> The LORD judges the peoples;
>> judge me, O LORD, according to my righteousness
>> and according to the integrity that is in me.
> Oh, let the evil of the wicked come to an end,
>> and may you establish the righteous—
> you who test the minds and hearts,
>> O righteous God!

The psalmist affirms that God will judge all the peoples, but then invites God to judge him, despite affirming that God tests the minds and hearts. It is a challenging and disturbing prayer: does every worshipper really want God to test his innermost motives? But time and again in the Psalms we meet this sort of prayer. The reciter or singer is thus involved in giving very active assent to the standards of life implied in the Psalms.

The closest analogy in Scripture to this affirmation of standards I think is found in Deuteronomy 27. There in a ceremony to be performed shortly after entry into the Promised Land, all the tribes stand before the Levites, who then pronounce curses on certain types of, mostly secret, sins.

> "Cursed be the man who makes a carved or cast metal image,
> . . . and sets it up in secret." . . .
>> "Cursed be anyone who dishonors his father or his mother." . . .
>> "Cursed be anyone who misleads a blind man on the road."
> (Deut. 27:15–16, 18)

After each curse, "all the people shall say, 'Amen'" (v. 18).

But even saying "amen" to a curse seems to me semi-passive,

when compared with reciting the psalm. When you pray a psalm, you are describing the actions you will take and what you will avoid. It is more like taking an oath or making a vow.

Austin pointed out that many remarks are much more than statements about facts, which are either true or false. We have already noted that promises change a situation by imposing obligations on the speaker and creating expectations in the listener. A promise is an example of a speech act. Wedding vows are speech acts too. The key words in a marriage ceremony are spoken publicly and before God. "I A take you B to be my wedded wife/ husband, to have and to hold from this day forward, for better for worse, for richer for poorer, in sickness and health, to love and to cherish, till death us do part."

One trusts that brides and grooms pronounce these words after careful thought beforehand and with complete sincerity on the big day. The words themselves transform their status: the two become man and wife. Thus the words are performative.[27] They change the situation. Speech-act philosophers have refined our understanding of illocutionary acts. According to Searle some utterances are directives: that is, they ask someone to do something.

> Save me, O God!
> > For the waters have come up to my neck. (Ps. 69:1)

Other speech acts are commissive: the speaker promises to do something.

> I said, "I will guard my ways,
> > that I may not sin with my tongue;
> I will guard my mouth with a muzzle,
> > so long as the wicked are in my presence." (Ps. 39:1)

Yet others are expressive: they express the emotion the speaker feels.

---

[27] P. Ramsey, "Liturgy and Ethics," *Journal of Religious Ethics* 7, no. 2 (1979): 139–71, argued that many liturgical remarks are performative; see 145–46.

> O Lord, all my longing is before you;
>> my sighing is not hidden from you. (Ps. 38:9)

And other speech acts are declarative: their very utterance effects a change.

> Ask of me, and I will make the nations your heritage,
>> and the ends of the earth your possession. (Ps. 2:8)

Searle, whose classification I have just used, points out that "often we do more than one of these things in the same utterance."[28] Using this categorization of speech acts, I suspect that one could say that praying the psalms involves the worshipper in many commissive speech acts: the psalms as prayers are really a series of vows. This is what sets them apart from other biblical texts with an ethical dimension.

One of the earliest writers to apply speech-act theory to the language of worship was Donald Evans in *The Logic of Self-Involvement*. Though he does not specifically discuss the language of the Psalms, his more general observations are most pertinent to our discussion. Evans does not use the more nuanced analysis of speech acts of Searle, but builds on Austin's simpler understanding of performative acts. He argues that most theological statements from a believer have a stronger or weaker commissive sense. This observation, I believe, aptly describes the situation of those praying the psalms. It is particularly pertinent to a study of the ethics of the Psalms.

Evans begins by noting that when God addresses mankind, he makes a commitment, and when man addresses God, there is a commitment in response.

> Similarly man does not (or does not merely) assert certain facts
> about God; he addresses God in the activity of worship, com-

[28] J. R. Searle, *Expression and Meaning* (Cambridge: Cambridge University Press, 1979), 29, quoted by R. S. Briggs, *Words in Action: Speech Act Theory and Biblical Interpretation* (Edinburgh: T&T Clark, 2001), 50.

mitting himself to God and expressing his attitude to God. In so far as God's self-revelation is a self-involving verbal activity ("His Word is claim and promise, gift and demand") and man's religious language is also a self-involving verbal activity ("obedient, thankful confession and prayer"), theology needs an outline of the various ways in which language is self-involving.[29]

Evans's book attempts to provide such an analysis of how the language of worship involves the worshipper. He adopts the terminology of Austin, the founder of speech-act theory, to define the character of worship language. Evans argues that this language falls into two main categories: commissives, in which the speaker commits himself to a course of action, and behabitives, in which an attitude is expressed. Typical commissives are *promise, pledge, accept, undertake, engage, threaten, swear loyalty, declare as policy*, and *take as wife*. Behabitives include such terms as *praise, thank, apologize, commend, blame, reprimand, glorify, worship, confess, welcome, protest*, and *accuse*.[30] Obviously both commissives and behabitives are found throughout the Psalter. For example:

> But I, through the abundance of your steadfast love,
>   will enter your house.
> I will bow down toward your holy temple
>   in the fear of you. (Ps. 5:7)

> I will give to the LORD the thanks due to his righteousness,
>   and I will sing praise to the name of the LORD, the Most
>   High. (Ps. 7:17)

Evans says that statements like "I promise/pledge" "are Commissive performatives, for the speaker *commits* himself in more than a verbal way. They have a 'content,' for the speaker is

---

[29] Donald D. Evans, *The Logic of Self-Involvement: A Philosophical Study of Everyday Language with Special Reference to the Christian Use of Language about God as Creator* (London: SCM, 1963), 14.
[30] Ibid., 29.

undertaking to behave in a specified way in the future; for example, he is undertaking to 'return this book tomorrow.'"[31]

God's promises are commissives. For example:

> I will tell of the decree:
> The LORD said to me, "You are my Son;
>   today I have begotten you.
> Ask of me, and I will make the nations your heritage,
>   and the ends of the earth your possession." (Ps. 2:7–8)

> Because he holds fast to me in love, I will deliver him;
>   I will protect him, because he knows my name. (Ps. 91:14)

These divine commitments evoke a human response. In fact many of the psalms quote divine promises in the psalmists' prayer and praise. Following Austin's terminology, Evans calls sentiments such as "I thank you," "we praise thee, O Lord," and "I apologize" behabitives,

> since they related the speaker to another person in the context of human *behaviour* and social relations, without being strongly Commissive. The speaker implies that he has certain attitudes in relation to the person whom he addresses, or towards what he is talking about. In saying, "I thank you," I imply (but do not report) that I am grateful to you; In saying, "I apologize for my behaviour," I imply (but do not report), that I have an unfavourable attitude towards my behaviour. Behabitives imply attitudes.[32]

Evans argues that since most language about God is either commissive or behabitive, it is therefore self-involving. Self-involvement is particularly evident in first-person utterances.

> Where *I* report my attitude in the present tense, my utterance is rarely a mere report, equivalent to *your* report of my attitude. It

---

[31] Ibid., 32.
[32] Ibid., 34–35.

tends to *commit* me to the pattern of behaviour to which I am referring; it has a forward reference to behaviour for which I am the responsible agent, not merely an observer.[33]

Many psalms illustrate this. For example:

> Oh, magnify the LORD with me,
> and let us exalt his name together!

> I sought the LORD, and he answered me
> and delivered me from all my fears.
> Those who look to him are radiant,
> and their faces shall never be ashamed. (Ps. 34:3–5)

> I waited patiently for the LORD;
> he inclined to me and heard my cry.
> He drew me up from the pit of destruction,
> out of the miry bog,
> and set my feet upon a rock,
> making my steps secure.
> He put a new song in my mouth,
> a song of praise to our God.
> Many will see and fear,
> and put their trust in the LORD. (Ps. 40:1–3)

Many remarks that on first sight seem to be mere statements of fact, constatives, within the context of worship have clearly performative force. According to the Old Testament, Evans observes, "man in general is created with a role as nature's steward and God's articulate worshipper. In the biblical context, to say, 'God is my Creator' is to acknowledge the *role* which God has assigned."[34] To say "I acknowledge you as my king" or "You are my king" is to express a strong commitment.[35] The so-called enthronement psalms offer many examples of this.

---

[33] Ibid., 119.
[34] Ibid., 155.
[35] Ibid., 52–53.

For the LORD is a great God,
>   and a great King above all gods. (Ps. 95:3)

The LORD reigns, let the earth rejoice;
>   let the many coastlands be glad! (Ps. 97:1)

The LORD reigns; let the peoples tremble!
>   He sits enthroned upon the cherubim; let the earth quake!
>   (Ps. 99:1)

These "Commissives are utterances in which the speaker commits himself to future patterns of more-than-merely-verbal behaviour."[36]

Even remarks like "God is holy" in a song of praise to God are more than a statement of God's attribute of holiness. They express a certain sense of awe in the worshipper.

> In the biblical context, to say, "God is glorious," or "God is holy" is to worship God; it is to express an attitude. As an expression of attitude, the utterance is both performative and expressive:
>   . . . .The words are used performatively to perform an act of praise and to commit oneself to various attitudes of supreme and exclusive devotion.[37]

Andreas Wagner makes a similar point. In the Old Testament, he says, "every confession of faith in Yahweh carries with it obligations. What is expressed in the sentence following Deut. 6:4 may be implied in all confessions of faith in Yahweh." Deuteronomy 6:4 runs, "Hear, O Israel: The LORD our God, the LORD is one." It continues in verse 5, "You shall love the LORD your God with all your heart and with all your soul and with all your might." Wagner explains that in confessing God's uniqueness, a person commits himself to God: "In the act of confession are embedded obligations, which one in and through confessing accepts for

---

[36] Ibid., 57.
[37] Ibid., 183.

oneself. Confessing faith in Yahweh means loving him and doing all that is according to his will."[38] Psalm 104 fits this analysis well. It begins:

> Bless the LORD, O my soul!
>> O LORD my God, you are very great!
> You are clothed with splendor and majesty,
>> covering yourself with light as with a garment,
>> stretching out the heavens like a tent. (vv. 1–2)

Then in language reminiscent of Genesis 1 the psalm recounts God's creative acts, including his provision of food for humans (vv. 3–30). This recounting evokes the outburst:

> O LORD, how manifold are your works!
>> In wisdom have you made them all;
>> the earth is full of your creatures. (Ps. 104:24)

These recollections of God's work in creation then motivate a strong commitment on the part of the psalmist.

> I will sing to the LORD as long as I live;
>> I will sing praise to my God while I have being.
> May my meditation be pleasing to him,
>> for I rejoice in the LORD.
> Let sinners be consumed from the earth,
>> and let the wicked be no more!
> Bless the LORD, O my soul!
> Praise the LORD! (Ps. 104:33–35)

Evans is quite correct to insist that "in the biblical context, the utterance 'God is my Creator' is profoundly self-involving."[39] His further point that the use of the present tense also has implications for future action is also important in singing the psalms.

---

[38] Andreas Wagner, *Sprechakte und Sprechaktanalyse im Alten Testament*, BZAW 253 (Berlin: de Gruyter, 1997), 215 (my trans.).

[39] Evans, *The Logic of Self-Involvement*, 160.

Where *I* report my attitude in the present tense, my utterance is rarely a mere report, equivalent to *your* report of my attitude. It tends to *commit* me to the pattern of behaviour to which I am referring; it has a forward reference to behaviour for which I am the responsible agent, not merely an observer.[40]

Again many passages from the Psalms could be cited to support Evans's contention. For example Psalm 116 begins,

I love the LORD, because he has heard
    my voice and my pleas for mercy. (v. 1)

Then after an extended account of how God has answered his prayer, the psalmist promises,

I will pay my vows to the LORD
    in the presence of all his people,
in the courts of the house of the LORD,
    in your midst, O Jerusalem.
Praise the LORD! (vv. 18–19)

A similar pattern is discernible in Psalm 118.

To sum up, singing or praying the psalms is a performative, typically a commissive, act: saying these solemn words to God alters one's relationship in a way that mere listening does not. This is not a new insight: St. Paul saw confession of faith as altering one's status before God: "If you confess with your mouth that Jesus is Lord and believe in your heart that God raised him from the dead, you will be saved. For with the heart one believes and is justified, and with the mouth one confesses and is saved" (Rom. 10:9–10).

Paul's argument may be applied to the Psalms. Throughout the Psalter one is confessing that the Lord is God, and as the Psalms often insist, this is supposed to be a confession that comes

---

[40] Ibid., 119. Wagner, 98, notes that explicitly performative utterances in Hebrew are generally put in the first person perfect.

from a pure and sincere heart. And it is certainly salvation that the Psalmist seeks: time and again he pleads to God to save him, to deliver him, to hear his prayer, and so on. Whether or not this always occurs is not my purpose to discuss now. I simply want to draw out some of the similarities between taking an oath, making a vow, confessing faith, and praying the psalms. I think these parallels may help us to see how powerful the commitment is that the psalms demand of their user. In singing the psalms, one is actively committing oneself to following the God-approved life. This is what we are doing singing the psalms.

CHAPTER 2

Praying the Psalms[1]

In the previous chapter I focused on the origin of the Psalter and the impact of speech-act theory for understanding it. But if we stop there, we miss the main point of the Psalms: they are designed to be prayed. This has been recognized down the ages, but let me just give the opinion of two well-known European theologians. John Calvin wrote, "Here is prescribed in the most exact manner how we may offer acceptably the sacrifice of praises, which God declareth to be most precious in his sight."[2] And more recently Dietrich Bonhoeffer wrote, "The only way to understand the Psalms is on your knees, the whole congregation praying the words of the Psalms with all its strength."[3]

I am sure if one searched further one could find exhortations to pray the psalms from many more great theologians, but despite this, in many parts of the church the Psalms are woefully neglected. At one seminary in Britain that I visited, they were not even on the syllabus to be studied. So in this chapter I will offer some reasons for praying all the psalms regularly.

I should like you to travel in your imagination to Jerusalem. When you arrive there in the Old City of Jerusalem, there is one place you cannot miss: the Dome of the Rock with its shiny golden dome and beautiful mosaics. It stands where the Jewish temple stood until its destruction by the Romans in AD 70. It is still a most sacred place for the Jews, and devout Jews will not walk on the temple mount, but in peaceful times Christian pilgrims are allowed to visit it. As you walk among the beautiful buildings,

---

[1] First presented at Nairobi Evangelical Graduate School of Theology, February 22, 2006.
[2] John Calvin, *A Commentary on the Psalms of David* (Oxford: Tegg, 1840), 1:viii.
[3] Lecture on July 31, 1935, quoted in Edwin Robertson, *My Soul Finds Rest in God Alone* (Guildford: Eagle, 2001), 8.

you can picture all those who worshipped there before you, from Abraham and Isaac to Jesus and Paul. But the two biblical figures we most associate with the Jerusalem temple are David and Solomon. Solomon of course built the first temple, while David wrote many of the psalms that were used there.

For nearly a thousand years the priests and the Levites and lay people too sang the psalms in the Jerusalem temple. The Jews also used them in their synagogues and homes. It was traditional to sing Psalms 113–18 at the Passover meal. We know that Jesus used these psalms at the Last Supper, for the Gospels mention it in passing. Matthew 26:30 says "And when they had sung a hymn they went out to the Mount of Olives." The hymn Jesus and his disciples sang at this point, just after the meal, comprised Psalms 115–18. When you next pray Psalm 118, remember that Jesus prayed it just before he went out to face his death. Here are a few verses:

> Out of my distress I called on the LORD;
>   the LORD answered me and set me free.
> The LORD is on my side; I will not fear.
>   What can man do to me? . . .
>
> I shall not die, but I shall live,
>   and recount the deeds of the LORD. . . .
>
> Open to me the gates of righteousness,
>   that I may enter through them
>   and give thanks to the LORD. . . .
> The stone that the builders rejected
>   has become the cornerstone. (Ps. 118:5–6, 17, 19, 22)

It is quite likely that Jesus and his disciples knew the psalms by heart, for we next hear Jesus reciting them on the cross. He quoted Psalm 22:1, "My God, my God, why have you forsaken me?" A bit later, just before he died he quoted Psalm 31:5, "Into your hand I commit my spirit" (Luke 23:46). It has been suggested that our Lord was just praying his way through the Psalms as he hung on the cross. As I shall say later, this would have been a very appropriate thing to do, for so many of the early psalms are the prayers of a good man suffering and crying to God for help.

The early church continued the practice of praying and singing the psalms. St. Paul tells the Ephesians, "Be filled with the Spirit, addressing one another in psalms . . . , singing and making melody to the Lord with all your heart" (Eph. 5:18–19). The apostle says much the same to the Colossians (3:16). If we turn to the book of Revelation, we are privileged to hear some of the songs of the saints in heaven, which too seem to be based on the Psalms.

Move on a couple of centuries and meet Athanasius, the great African theologian who saved the church from denying the divinity of Christ. He wrote a marvelous letter about the Psalms to a man named Marcellinus. The gist of the letter is that the Psalms are the best part of the Bible, and we should use them for our prayers whatever our situation may be because there is a psalm that suits our every need. Below are a few sentences from this wonderful letter:

> Whatever your particular need or trouble, from this same book you can select a form of words to fit it, so that you do not merely hear and then pass on, but learn the way to remedy your ill. . . . The Psalms . . . show you how to set about repenting and with what words your penitence may be expressed. . . . The Psalms not only exhort us to be thankful, they also provide us with fitting words to say. We are told, too, by other writers that all who would live godly in Christ must suffer persecution; and here again the Psalms supply words with which both those who flee persecution and those who suffer under it may suitably address themselves to God, and it does the same for those who have been rescued from it. We are bidden elsewhere in the Bible also to bless the Lord and to acknowledge Him: here in the Psalms we are shown the way to do it, and with what sort of words His majesty may meetly be confessed. In fact, under all the circumstances of life, we shall find that these divine songs suit ourselves and meet our own souls' need at every turn.[4]

---

[4] Athanasius, *On the Incarnation*, with appendix "On the Interpretation of the Psalms," ed. and trans. a religious of C.S.M.V. (New York: St Vladimir's Seminary Press, 1977), 103–4.

The later church took Athanasius's advice to heart. When Saint Benedict set up monasteries in about AD 600, he prescribed the reciting of psalms at the eight times of prayer each day. In this way the monks prayed every psalm at least once a week. As noted in chapter 1, in the Middle Ages, before the age of printing, the only piece of the Bible a lay person was likely to have was a copy of the Psalms. I am told that is still the case in southern Ethiopia today.

The Protestant Reformers were just as keen on the use of the Psalms. Again, Luther described the Psalter as a mini-Bible, which sums up the whole message of the Scriptures. John Calvin wrote, "Whatever may serve to encourage us when we are about to pray to God, is taught us in this book."[5] In many Reformed churches that followed Calvin's teaching, only the psalms, or hymns that were a close paraphrase of the psalms, could be sung in church. Other songs or hymns were forbidden. In the Church of England prayer book the Psalms are divided up so that, on average, five may be said or sung each day and every psalm is thereby prayed once a month.

But from the eighteenth century this use of the Psalms in English-speaking Protestant churches began to decline. Men like Isaac Watts, Charles Wesley, John Newton, and others in the evangelical revival wrote very good hymns that were easier to sing than the psalms. In their day of course people continued to pray and sing the psalms, but as time went on, the use of the Psalms began to die out. So today many churches in Britain and America never use the Psalms at all, and some seminaries do not even make study of the Psalms part of their curriculum.

Now I am not against hymns or modern worship songs. Some of them are great, but if we sing only them, we will have a very limited experience of worship, indeed a harmful imbalance in our praying and singing. So in the rest of this chapter I want to offer some reasons why we ought to pray the psalms regularly as Jesus and the apostles did, and as the Christian church did as well for about eighteen centuries.

---

[5] Calvin, *A Commentary on the Psalms of David*, 1:viii.

Psalms of Praise

First of all, the Psalms teach us to praise God. The Hebrew word which is translated "Psalms" is *tehillim*, which means "praises." The Psalms show us how to praise God for all his goodness to us.

Praise for Creation

Psalm 104 praises God for his wisdom in creation.

> Bless the LORD, O my soul!
>> O LORD my God, you are very great!
> You are clothed with splendor and majesty,
>> covering yourself with light as with a garment,
>> stretching out the heavens like a tent. (vv. 1–2)

> He set the earth on its foundations,
>> so that it should never be moved. (v. 5)

The psalmist goes on to mention the creation of the seas, the mountains, the birds, the plants, man, the moon, and the sun, and then he exclaims,

> O LORD, how manifold are your works!
>> In wisdom have you made them all. (v. 24)

Praise for Salvation

The Psalms praise God for salvation. God's rescue of his people from slavery in Egypt through the exodus was the supreme saving act in the Old Testament, and many psalms celebrate that: for example, 105, 106, 115, and 136. You may be tempted to say that praising God for the exodus is not relevant to us, but of course it is. The New Testament sees Christ's death on the cross for us as the new exodus. So when we praise God in these psalms, we remember not only the first exodus from Egypt but, moreover, the second exodus whereby we were saved from the slavery of sin.

Praise for Answered Prayer

The Psalms give us words to praise God when our prayers are answered. Like the nine lepers in Luke's Gospel it is easy for us to forget to thank God for answered prayer or to thank him too swiftly and casually. But the Psalms teach us how we ought to respond to his goodness. Psalm 30 is a beautiful example.

> I will extol you, O LORD, for you have drawn me up.
>> and have not let my foes rejoice over me.
> O LORD my God, I cried to you for help,
>> and you have healed me. . . .
>
> Sing praises to the LORD, O you his saints,
>> and give thanks to his holy name.
> For his anger is but for a moment,
>> and his favor is for a lifetime.
> Weeping may tarry for the night,
>> but joy comes with the morning. (vv. 1–2, 4–5)

Praise for the Law

The Psalms also praise God for the law. C. S. Lewis thought that Psalm 19 is the most beautiful of all the psalms, and it is this psalm that compares the law to the sun. As the sun provides light and heat to sustain life on earth, so

> the law of the LORD is perfect,
>> reviving the soul. (Ps. 19:7)

The longest psalm, Psalm 119, is all about the law. It is divided into twenty-two sections, each section consisting of eight verses, all of which begin with the letter of the Hebrew alphabet for that section. Why does the psalmist go through the Hebrew alphabet in this way? I think it is to show that the law is absolutely perfect, and this is his poetic way of making that point. He wants us, like him, to say,

Oh how I love your law!
    It is my meditation all the day. (Ps. 119:97)

A Word on the Arrangement

Before we leave the psalms of praise, we should note something about the arrangement of them. Hymns of praise are not very frequent at the beginning of the book, but as you read on, you will find more and more of them. It is as though the more you pray, the more you will realize God's goodness. In fact the book closes with five great hymns of praise, the last being the most spectacular of all, Psalm 150. Here we are given a glimpse of what heaven will be like.

Praise the LORD!
Praise God in his sanctuary;
    praise him in his mighty heavens!
Praise him for his mighty deeds;
    praise him according to his excellent greatness!

Praise him with trumpet sound;
    praise him with lute and harp!
Praise him with tambourine and dance;
    praise him with strings and pipe!
Praise him with sounding cymbals;
    praise him with loud clashing cymbals!
Let everything that has breath praise the LORD!
Praise the LORD!

Psalms of Lament

I have said that the Hebrew title of the book of Psalms, *tehillim*, actually means "praises." So what kind of psalms would you expect to be the most common in the book? Presumably cheerful upbeat songs of praise. But if that is the answer you gave, you would be wrong. Hymns of praise do dominate the end of the Psalter, as I have just said, but in the book as a whole the most common type of psalm is the lament. A lament is a psalm in which the writer prays that God will deliver him from some crisis: sometimes his enemies, sometimes defeat in battle, sometimes a life-threatening illness. In these situations the psalmist often seems to think that God has deserted him. Perhaps the best known of these laments is Psalm 22, which begins, "My God, my God, why have you forsaken me?"

A somewhat shorter lament is Psalm 13.

> How long, O LORD? Will you forget me forever?
>   How long will you hide your face from me?
> How long must I take counsel in my soul
>   and have sorrow in my heart all the day?
> How long shall my enemy be exalted over me?
>
> Consider and answer me, O LORD my God;
>   light up my eyes, lest I sleep the sleep of death,
> lest my enemy say, "I have prevailed over him,"
>   lest my foes rejoice because I am shaken. (vv. 1–4)

The psalmist was in real trouble. He was being attacked by his enemies, and he was doubting whether God still cared for him. He worried that his enemies would realize how shaky his faith was and would gloat over this loss of faith.

But like most laments, this one suddenly changes key, and it ends on a note of confidence and praise.

> But I have trusted in your steadfast love;
>   my heart shall rejoice in your salvation.
> I will sing to the LORD,
>   because he has dealt bountifully with me. (vv. 5–6)

Though laments usually end on a note of hope, several do not. Though at some point they may express hope, the psalmist sometimes reverts to despair at the end. His glimmer of faith seems extinguished. But there is one psalm that contains no expression of hope or faith anywhere. The first and last few verses give us the flavor of it.

O LORD, God of my salvation;
  I cry out day and night before you.
Let my prayer come before you;
  incline your ear to my cry!

For my soul is full of troubles,
  and my life draws near to Sheol. . . .

Your wrath has swept over me;
  your dreadful assaults destroy me.
They surround me like a flood all day long;
  they close in on me together.
You have caused my beloved and my friend to shun me;
  my companions have become darkness. (Ps. 88:1–3, 16–18)

Can Christians use such psalms? Should we not be giving thanks in all circumstances? Are such songs appropriate to people of faith, particularly for use in public worship? These are the sorts of questions the psalms of lament raise.

I want to give four theological reasons for using the laments, and two practical ones.

Theological Reasons for the Laments

1. *The lament psalms are some of the most quoted in the New Testament.* Take Psalm 69 for example. It is second only to Psalm 22 as the most quoted psalm in the New Testament. Psalm 69 begins:

Save me, O God!
  For the waters have come up to my neck.
I sink in deep mire,
  where there is no foothold;
I have come into deep waters,
  and the flood sweeps over me. (Ps. 69:1–2)

Quoted in John 15:25 is verse 4:

> More in number than the hairs of my head
> > are those who hate me without cause.

Quoted in John 2:17 and Romans 15:3 is verse 9:

> For zeal for your house has consumed me,
> > and the reproaches of those who reproach you have fallen
> > > on me.

Quoted in Romans 11:9 are verses 22–23:

> Let their own table before them become a snare;
> > and when they are at peace, let it become a trap.
> Let their eyes be darkened, so that they cannot see,
> > and make their loins tremble continually.

And quoted in Acts 1:20 is verse 25:

> May their camp be a desolation;
> > let no one dwell in their tents.

There are many allusions to this psalm in other passages too.

2. *Jesus prayed these lament psalms.* If he was praying one psalm after another during his crucifixion, as I have suggested, he must have prayed about a dozen laments by the time he reached Psalm 22, one of the most powerful of all laments. And the Gospels tell us that he did pray that one.

3. *The book of Revelation includes one of the prayers of the dead martyrs in heaven that is based on the lament psalms.* In Revelation 6:9–10 John says, "I saw under the altar the souls of those who had been slain for the word of God and for the witness they had borne. They cried out with a loud voice, 'O Sovereign Lord, holy and true, how long before you will judge and avenge our blood on those who dwell on the earth?'" This prayer is in fact based on three psalms: Psalms 94:3; 79:10; and 119:84.

4. *The early church prayed these psalms.* The great African

theologian Athanasius said the following about the use of these psalms:

> If you are persecuted by your own family and opposed by many, say Psalm 3. . . . When you see the wicked wanting to ensnare you and you wish your prayer to reach God's ears, then wake up early and sing Psalm 5. . . . When again, you need to pray against your enemies and those who straiten you, Psalms 17, 86, 88 and 140 will all meet your need. . . . Pay no attention either to the weakness of your humanity or to the brazenness of their attack, but cry unceasingly to God using Psalm 28.[6]

I hope this is sufficient to show that we ought to use these psalms in our private prayers and in public worship. But let me add two practical and pastoral reasons why we should use them.

Practical Reasons for the Laments

1. *Not everyone who comes to church is full of joy and happiness.* There are many who come with great burdens, both physical and spiritual: sickness, marital problems, financial difficulties, pressure at work, even harassment and persecution. Old age brings all sorts of problems with it. Often people can see no way out, and they need to be allowed to cry out to God in their distress, just as Job did and Jesus himself did. Sufferers may pray the laments with hope that they will be able to say not only, "How long, O LORD? Will you forget me forever?" but also,

> I will sing to the LORD,
>> because he has dealt bountifully with me. (Ps. 13:1, 6)

2. *By praying these psalms those who have no problems and difficulties in their lives can learn to sympathize with those in trouble and pray for those who are suffering or persecuted.* The eminent American scholar James Mays has said,

---

[6] Athanasius, *On the Incarnation*, 107–9.

There may be no trouble for the present that corresponds to the tribulations described in the psalms, but do we need to do more than call the roll of such places as El Salvador, South Africa, China to remember that there are sisters and brothers whose trials could be given voice in our recitation of the psalms?[7]

Mays wrote this several years ago, but there are still plenty of other places in the world where Christians are under pressure, particularly in the Muslim world, in China, and in India. The news media frequently remind us of the problems of Africa: war, corrupt government, AIDS, drought, and famine. Helpless victims of these hardships need our prayers.

The early church prayed the Lord's Prayer three times a day, including the petitions

Your kingdom come,
your will be done
    on earth as it is in heaven. (Matt. 6:10)

That is a prayer that God will reign and that all evils will come to an end. So is that other short prayer of the early church, *Maranatha*, "Come Lord Jesus." Early Christians prayed for his second coming to bring an end to all their troubles. So let us use the laments to give more depth and sympathy to our prayers for our brothers and sisters in need.

Laments versus Violence

But a problem is sometimes raised about the laments. Some of them seem too vicious for Christians to use. Should a Christian really say, for example, these words?

Break the arm of the wicked and evildoer;
    call his wickedness to account till you find none. (Ps. 10:15)

---

[7] Lecture, April 2, 1991, quoted by J. Clinton McCann Jr., *A Theological Introduction to the Book of Psalms* (Nashville: Abingdon Press, 1993), 117.

Let me answer by making three short points. For a fuller discussion, I suggest the excellent book by Erich Zenger, *A God of Vengeance?*

1. It is surely better to pray to God to punish the wicked than to do it yourself. Praying the laments breaks the circle of violence instead of perpetuating it.

2. These prayers to God to judge the wicked are an expression of hope in God's justice. None of us wants to see the wicked get away with it. Human justice is very imperfect. Few sinners are apprehended by the police, and some who come to trial are acquitted, though everyone knows their guilt. Throughout the world the rich exploit the poor, and we are powerless to do anything about it. Psalms of lament call on God to stop injustice and exploitation and oppression. By calling on God to intervene, the psalmist or the one praying the psalms is affirming that God is the utterly fair and all-knowing Judge. To those suffering, such laments are a message of hope: God will not let the wicked get away with it forever.

3. But these psalms do more: Zenger explains that these psalms

> uncover the mechanisms of violence as actions and strategies emanating from concrete human beings and institutions. . . . These psalms can and will make obvious the web of violence presented, especially for the weak, the suffering, and those under attack. . . . With their concrete expressions of fear and pain, they bring that pain to the center of ordinary religious and social life. They are the expression of that sensitivity to suffering that is constitutive for biblical piety, and for any way of life that is shaped by the Bible.[8]

To put Zenger's point more simply: if we care about the suffering of our fellow Christians, we should pray these psalms.

There is a Christian charity in Britain called the Barnabas Fund, whose purpose is to channel aid to suffering Christians. The Barnabas Fund also issues a daily prayer diary to encourage

---

[8] Erich Zenger, *A God of Vengeance? Understanding the Psalms of Divine Wrath*, trans. Linda M. Maloney (Louisville: Westminster John Knox, 1996), 74–75.

prayer for persecuted Christians. One typical entry describes Ribqa Masih, a twenty-two-year-old Pakistani Christian who was drugged, kidnapped, and raped by three Muslim men. They also threatened to kill her and her whole family unless she recited the Islamic creed. Various other horrific details follow in the diary.

How does one pray in such a case? I at least have found the lament psalms a help.

Penitential Psalms

So far we have looked at psalms of praise and psalms of lament. There is a yet a third category I should like to mention: the seven penitential psalms, namely, 6, 32, 38, 51, 102, 130, and 143. Some of these could also be classified as lament psalms, but they are called penitential psalms because they have traditionally been used for self-examination and confession of sins and are most often used in Lent and Holy Week. Lent commemorates Jesus's forty days of fasting and prayer in the wilderness and leads up to Good Friday and Easter. So these penitential psalms are most appropriate for that season, when Christians are encouraged to fast and pray and to reexamine their lives so that they may more closely follow Christ.

The greatest and most famous of the penitential prayers is Psalm 51. According to its title it was composed by David after he had been condemned by Nathan the prophet for committing adultery with Bathsheba and murdering her husband. Although few people sin that badly, all of us have sinned, indeed keep on sinning in various ways, so we all need to confess our failings to God. We learn from David how to do so. The psalm begins,

> Have mercy on me, O God,
>   according to your steadfast love;
> according to your abundant mercy
>   blot out my transgressions. (Ps. 51:1)

David knows he has no claim on God's kindness: he has sinned far too much. So he appeals simply to God's "mercy," "steadfast love," and "abundant mercy." These three terms are borrowed from the golden calf story, when all Israel sinned. Yet God, in response to Moses's prayer, forgave his wayward people. Here David asks God to show the same mercy to him as he showed to Israel in Moses's day.

He continues to describe his offenses in the blackest terms he can: he does not minimize his sin. They are "transgressions," "sin," "evil," "iniquity." He has been a sinner from the moment he was conceived in his mother's womb. His sin is so indelible that only God can wash it out. So he prays that God will wash him, blot out his sin, cleanse him, purge him. If God washes him, he will be "whiter than snow." He prays for forgiveness so that he may declare God's goodness to others.

> Then I will teach transgressors your ways,
>   and sinners will return to you. (Ps. 51:13)

In a remarkable way the penitential psalms capture the gospel message, "If we confess our sins, he is faithful and just to forgive us our sins and to cleanse us from all unrighteousness" (1 John 1:9).

One thing that comes out of this psalm is that not only is David praying for himself, but because he is king his actions represent and affect the whole nation. That is why he alludes to the golden calf episode when all Israel was caught up in idolatry. That is why St. John says, "If *we* confess *our* sins." That is why Jesus taught us to pray "Forgive *us our* debts," not "forgive *me my* debts." So just as we can pray the lament psalms even when we are not in deep trouble ourselves because we are praying them on behalf of those who are suffering, so we can use the penitential psalms in the same way. We may not have sinned as badly as David or have anything particular weighing on our conscience, but we may know that members of our family have sinned, or that there is sin in our church or in our community or in our nation. We can and should pray these prayers then, not only on our own behalf but on behalf of the wider circles of life to which we belong.

Some people are very keen on the church making apologies for its past sins: for anti-Semitism, or its support of slavery, or whatever sin they light on. While I am not opposed to such gestures (Pope John Paul's apologies when he went to Israel deeply moved the Jews), I think our first duty is to express our penitence to God for the sins of our churches and our societies, and to pray that he will change people's thoughts and ways. Like Ezra (9:6–15), Nehemiah (1:5–11; 9:16–37), and the psalmists we should take responsibility and confess not just our personal sins, but the sins of our society. The penitential psalms can be a vehicle of such remorse.

Messianic Psalms

The last group of psalms I want to talk about are the royal or messianic psalms. These include Psalms 2, 45, 72, 89, 110, 132, 144. On the face of it, these psalms are just about the king in Jerusalem, but Jews and Christians have usually seen them not just as historical but also as prophetic. Take Psalm 72 for example, entitled "Of Solomon." The psalmist, presumably David, prays:

> May he have dominion from sea to sea,
>   and from the River to the ends of the earth! . . .
> May all kings fall down before him,
>   all nations serve him! (vv. 8, 11)

Solomon never achieved this, nor could he have. Only David's greater son, the Christ,

> delivers the needy when he calls,
>   the poor and him who has no helper. (v. 12)

Now I have listed the most obviously royal and messianic psalms, but recently scholars have come to see that many more relate to this theme. It is clear that the psalms have not been arranged in a random order. They have been divided into five books, like the Mosaic Pentateuch (1–41, 42–72, 73–89, 90–106,

107–50). And usually there is a messianic psalm at the beginning
or end of a book, most obviously Psalms 2, 72, 89. As we have seen,
Psalm 72 has a very upbeat prophecy about the role of David's
son. But turn to the next book of the Psalms, 73–89, and we get
a very gloomy picture: everything is going wrong for Israel. And
it closes with the psalmist accusing God of breaking his promises
to David that his offspring would be established forever, and his
throne endure forever (Ps. 89:4, 38–45). He laments:

> How long, O Lord? Will you hide yourself forever?
> How long will your wrath burn like fire? (Ps. 89:46)

Clearly this psalm was written after the fall of Jerusalem,
when the city was sacked and its king taken into exile. Psalm 89
and the preceding ones were collected together after this exile and
reflect on the hopeless situation the Jews faced at the time. They
had no king, and their land was occupied by the Persians. They
asked themselves, has God forgotten his promises? The answer is
given in the next book of the Psalms, 90–106. This contains a number of psalms that declare that the Lord reigns. He is king over
Jerusalem; he is king over nature; he is king over the nations. And
surely as he is the almighty king, he can and will keep his promises.
One day David's greater son will reign. Hence we find in the last
book of the Psalms more messianic psalms looking forward to the
new David's reign (110, 132, 144).

But what will this new David be like? For a fuller description
we must look at the opening two psalms. Psalm 1 introduces us to
the righteous man who meditates on the law day and night and
shuns the company of the wicked. Psalm 2 introduces us to the
Davidic king to whom God says,

> You are my Son;
> today I have begotten you. (v. 7)

The two opening psalms thus give us sketches of two people, a
righteous man and a royal man. What the following psalms do is to

combine these two figures into one, a righteous royal person. Thus all the next forty psalms or so are headed "A Psalm of David." But they do not describe the glorious all-triumphant son of David of Psalms 2 and 72. They describe a suffering David. Psalm 3 has the title, "A Psalm of David, when he fled from Absalom his son." And its first verse reads:

> O LORD, how many are my foes!
>   Many are rising against me.

Psalm 13, another psalm of David, begins, "How long, O LORD? Will you forget me forever?" Psalm 22 is another psalm of David. Thus if we read the psalms in sequence, we get the message: the new son of David is going to have to suffer like the old David before his worldwide rule, described in Psalm 72, becomes a reality. The book of the Psalms looks forward thus to the Messiah suffering before he enters into glory. Jesus made this point to the disciples on the way to Emmaus. He said to them, "O foolish ones, and slow of heart to believe all that the prophets have spoken! Was it not necessary that the Christ should suffer these things and enter into his glory?" (Luke 24:25–26).

But there is one more thing we should see in these psalms. The righteous man of Psalm 1 and the suffering man of the following psalms is not just the son of David. He is the son of Adam. In Psalm 8 the psalmist asks, "What is man that you are mindful of him?" (v. 4). In other words, the person blessed in Psalm 1 is every righteous man or woman, for everyone is, theologically speaking, a descendant of Adam. Thus everyone can potentially receive the blessing promised in Psalm 1 if he avoids the wicked and meditates on the law. But it also follows that just as the royal righteous man will suffer, so other righteous people will suffer too before they enter into glory. As St. Peter puts it, "Rejoice insofar as you share Christ's sufferings, that you may also rejoice and be glad when his glory is revealed" (1 Pet. 4:13).

Conclusion

This chapter was entitled "Praying the Psalms." I hope I have convinced you that we should use the psalms as prayers, whether said or sung. I hope I have persuaded you that we should use all the psalms, not just the cheerful or sentimental ones that take our fancy. We need to expand the scope of our prayers to take in the hurts of our world, not just its joys. As Christians we are, like our Master, called to suffer before we enter glory. And if we are spared suffering ourselves, we should pray for those who do suffer, using the words the Holy Spirit has inspired in the Psalms.

So how do we pray them? I think Psalm 1 tells us: "On his law he meditates day and night." As I said earlier, the law referred to here is not just the law of Moses, but the law of David—that is, the book of the Psalms, which likewise is divided into five books. We are thus called to meditate on the Psalms day and night.

Now, I should point out that meditate is not a very clear translation of the Hebrew word *hagah*. This word is translated "plot" in the next psalm. It means "mumble, talk quietly." It is what you do when you read aloud. Nobody read silently in Bible times. Reading was always aloud. Of course few people in Bible times had any part of the Bible in written form: they memorized it and then recited it. This is how we should use the Psalms: read them out loud or recite them to ourselves. But we should also use them in family worship, with our spouse, and with our children. Deuteronomy says of the laws, "You shall teach them diligently to your children, and shall talk of them when you sit in your house, and when you walk by the way, and when you lie down, and when you rise" (Deut. 6:7). What Deuteronomy says of its laws applies just as well to the Psalms.

But I do not see why the Psalms should not also be used outside the family circle. The early church used them as St. Paul said, "addressing one another" in teaching and singing (Eph. 5:18; Col. 3:16). Let us use them in house groups and prayer circles. They were used in public worship by nearly all churches till the twentieth century. Is it not time our churches recovered this practice?

CHAPTER 3

Reading the Psalms Canonically[1]

The twentieth century saw two revolutions in approaches to reading the Psalms. At the beginning of the century scholarship generally regarded the Psalms as poems of personal devotion that were taken over for use in meditation or worship. Though many psalms had titles implying that they had been written by David or other luminaries, such as Asaph, most scholars around 1900 placed little store by these ascriptions, but supposed most of the psalms had been composed much later, some time between the exile and the Maccabean era.

The first revolution in twentieth-century Psalm study was introduced by Hermann Gunkel, *Die Psalmen* (1926), and was carried through by Sigmund Mowinckel, *The Psalms in Israel's Worship* (1962). Their method of form criticism is well known and set out in the standard textbooks. It involves classifying the psalms into different types—hymns, laments, wisdom psalms, and so on—and then suggesting possible *Sitze im Leben* for the different categories. These settings usually turned out to involve worship in the pre-exilic temple, though it was recognized that some psalms were composed in later times.

Both form critics and their immediate predecessors tended to view the Psalms as historical artifacts that shed light on their authors or the circumstances of their composition or their subsequent use. According to earlier critics[2] Psalm 46 might have

---

[1] First read in Rome in June 2005, and published as "Towards a Canonical Reading of the Psalms," in *Canon and Biblical Interpretation*, ed. Craig G. Bartholomew et al. (Milton Keynes: Paternoster, 2006), 331–51. Used with permission.

[2] "The miraculous deliverance of Jerusalem from the army of Sennacherib (B.C. 701) may be assigned as the occasion of the Psalms, with a probability which approaches certainty." A. F. Kirkpatrick,

reflected the lifting of a siege on Jerusalem in 701, while form critics appealed to Psalms 2 and 110 to illuminate royal coronation ceremonies, or to Psalms 93–100 to demonstrate that the autumn festival was the occasion of Yahweh's enthronement.[3] Commentaries on the Psalms thus tended to have a history-of-religions perspective rather than a theological focus.

It was also characteristic of these earlier approaches to read the psalms as individual poems or worship songs and to pay little attention to the collection as a whole and to its arrangement. Certain obvious groupings were noted, such as the Songs of Ascents or the Psalms of the Sons of Korah. It was often noted that Psalm 1 is an appropriate introduction to the Psalter as a whole, but the implications of its message for the whole were rarely touched on. Form criticism encouraged readers to compare psalms of the same genre, but seldom were the relationships between adjacent psalms in the Psalter explored.

All this began to change with the publication of Gerald Wilson's *The Editing of the Hebrew Psalter* (1985). This heralded the second revolution in twentieth-century Psalm study, which is the topic of this chapter. In the following I want first to explain Wilson's work and the way his method and insights have been developed especially by American scholarship. Then, second, I want to discuss the commentary of Frank-Lothar Hossfeld and Erich Zenger on Psalms 51–100. This is a major work in Herder's *Theologischer Kommentar zum Alten Testament* series, one of three volumes projected to cover the Psalter. Hossfeld and Zenger well illustrate the methods of canonical reading, so I will use their interpretation of one psalm to illustrate their approach to canonical reading of the Psalms. Then I shall conclude by reflecting on some of the problems that canonical readings raise: What is the historical context in which the Psalter was compiled? What difference do the psalm titles make to canonical interpretation?

The Book of Psalms (Cambridge: Cambridge University Press, 1902), 253; cf. Joseph A. Alexander, *The Psalms Translated and Explained* (1873; repr., Grand Rapids: Baker, 1975), 209.
[3] E.g., Sigmund Mowinckel, *The Psalms in Israel's Worship*, one-volume ed., trans. D. R. Ap-Thomas (Grand Rapids: Eerdmans, 2004), 61.

How does the total canonical context affect our understanding and appropriation of the Psalms? Are we talking simply of the Old Testament and New Testament canon of Scripture, or are we thinking of the church's use of the Psalms down the ages?

Wilson, *The Editing of the Hebrew Psalter*

The Editing of the Hebrew Psalter began life as a dissertation at Yale and, among others, it is dedicated to Brevard Childs, who, says Wilson, "taught me to respect the canon." This book has blazed a trail that many others have since followed and indeed tried to improve on. Though initially this pursuit was largely an American and Protestant project, it has been enthusiastically taken up by Catholic scholars in Europe, such as Lohfink, Hossfeld, Zenger, and Auwers.

However, though the arrangement of the Psalter has been discussed intensively only in the last two decades, earlier writers did make occasional observations on the topic. For example Rabbi Abbahu and Eusebius noted that it was association of ideas that linked the psalms, not chronology. Basil and Jerome noted that Psalm 1 seemed to serve as a title or introduction to the whole Psalter.[4] In his nineteenth-century commentary on the Psalms, Franz Delitzsch noted how consecutive psalms were linked together by key words. At the end of the century Benno Jacob, in an article on the sequence of the psalms (1898), noted some structural features of the Psalter, such as blessings at the beginning and end of books,[5] the placing of acrostic psalms,[6] and the gathering of prayers of the individual at the end of books.[7] But Delitzsch and Jacob were voices crying in the wilderness. For most of the nineteenth and twentieth centuries scholarly interest was focused on the earliest form of the text, its genesis and meaning, not on

---

[4] Jean-Marie Auwers, *La composition littéraire du psautier: Un état de la question* (Paris: Gabalda, 2000), 12–14.

[5] Pss. 1:1; 2:12; 41:1; 72:17; 89:15; 106:3; 144:15.

[6] Psalms 111–12 after three Davidic psalms; Psalm 119 after the Passover Hallel; Psalm 145 at end of third and last Davidic collection, 138–45.

[7] Psalms 38–41, 69–71, 86, 88, 102, 140–43.

the final or canonical form. But when Wilson published his book on the editing of the Psalter, final-form readings of Old Testament narrative were very much in vogue.[8] So, far from being ignored, Wilson's work initiated a new wave of interest in final-form and canonical readings of the Psalms.

The Editing of the Hebrew Psalter begins by reviewing evidence from Mesopotamia that collections of temple songs were arranged according to a variety of criteria, such as genre, deity addressed, and similar phrases.[9] The next two chapters review the evidence of the Qumran Psalm manuscripts to see whether there are discernible patterns in the arrangement of the psalms. Among these manuscripts there seems to be considerable fluidity in the order of the last book of the Psalter, leading Wilson to agree with those who think that this section of the Psalter may not have been canonized till very late.[10]

The last two chapters of *The Editing of the Hebrew Psalter* are the most original. In the first of these Wilson asks whether the psalm titles give any insight into the principles of arrangement. He does not think this is the case, as a title describes the particular psalm it heads, not a group of psalms. Nevertheless psalms with similar titles do seem to be grouped together, for example, the psalms of David (e.g., 3–41, 51–65, 68–70, 138–45); but common authorship is not obviously an overriding factor in the arrangement, or else all the psalms of David would have been grouped together. Similarly one might have expected all the psalms of Asaph or the sons of Korah to have been grouped together.[11] Only in the case of the Songs of Ascents (Psalms 120–34) does a common generic title seem to have led to their all being put together.

More revealing of editorial purpose, Wilson suggests, are the conclusions to each of the five books of the Psalms. Each book ends with a benediction, for example:

---

[8] E.g., Robert Alter, *The Art of Biblical Narrative* (New York: Basic Books, 1981), and Meir Sternberg, *The Poetics of Biblical Narrative* (Bloomington: Indiana University Press, 1985).
[9] Gerald H. Wilson, *The Editing of the Hebrew Psalter* (Chico, CA: Scholars Press, 1985), 13–61.
[10] Ibid., 93–121.
[11] Ibid., 155–73.

Blessed be the LORD, the God of Israel,
>   from everlasting to everlasting!
>   Amen and Amen. (Ps. 41:13)

Blessed be the LORD forever!
>   Amen and Amen. (Ps. 89:52; cf. 72:18–19; 106:48)

The Psalter concludes with a group of psalms that amount to an extended doxology to the whole work (146–50).[12] Wilson notes that the first psalm appears to be an introduction to the whole collection, while Psalm 2 introduces the first book of the Psalms (2–41).[13] The Davidic titles, by identifying David as the speaker, allow the reader praying or meditating on the psalms to put himself in David's shoes.[14]

In his final chapter Wilson begins to explore the theological implications of recognizing an editorial purpose in the arrangement of the Psalter.

> The effect of the editorial fixation of the first psalm as an introduction to the whole Psalter is subtly to alter how the reader views and appropriates the psalms collected there. The emphasis is now on meditation rather than cultic performance; private, individual use over public, communal participation. In a strange transformation, Israel's words of response to her God have now become the Word of God to Israel.[15]

The division of the Psalter is also significant according to Wilson. He notes that at the seams of the first three books (Psalms 1–41, 42–72, 73–89) are psalms about the Davidic covenant, recalling God's promise to David that he would be the founder of an eternal dynasty (see Pss. 2:7–9; 41:11–12; 72:17; 89:19–37). But whereas the references to the Davidic covenant are quite positive

---

[12] Ibid., 182–86.
[13] Ibid., 173.
[14] "The final effect within the Psalter has been to provide a hermeneutical approach to the use of the psalms by the *individual*. As David, so every man!" Wilson, *The Editing of the Hebrew Psalter*, 173.
[15] Ibid., 206.

in the first two books, Psalm 89 laments that God does not appear
to be keeping his promises.

> You have renounced the covenant with your servant;
> you have defiled his crown in the dust. (v. 39)

And the psalm ends with an appeal to God to remember his
promises.

> Lord, where is your steadfast love of old,
> which by your faithfulness you swore to David? (v. 49)

This dismal close to book 3 of the Psalter is answered by book
4 (Psalms 90–106), which Wilson declares to be "the editorial 'center' of the final form of the Hebrew Psalter."[16] The answer to the
nonfulfillment of the Davidic promises is that "the LORD reigns"
(Pss. 93:1; 96:10; 97:1; 99:1). Back in the time of Moses (Ps. 90:1)
the Lord was Israel's refuge. He still is, and Israel must continue
to trust in him. Two groups of Davidic psalms are found in book
5 (108–10, 138–45). Among the Songs of Ascents (Psalms 120–34)
is one (132) that celebrates the Davidic covenant, but Wilson is not
sure that this is a reaffirmation of the Davidic promises. He seems
to think that though this might have been the conviction of those
who compiled the Songs of Ascents, this is not the view of the final
editor, who wanted readers to put their trust in Yahweh the eternal
king, not in a temporal earthly one.[17]

Wilson's work opened a new era in Psalm study, and the valid-
ity of many of his observations has been widely acknowledged.
The importance of Psalms 1 and 2 for the theology of the Psalter
is now accepted: the first gives a wisdom slant to the collection,
and the second draws attention to the role of the king. Whether
the promises to the house of David were understood messianically
by the Psalter's editor is still a matter of contention. Wilson uti-
lized the titles of the psalms as a means of classifying and group-

---

[16] Ibid., 215.
[17] Ibid., 225, 228.

ing them, but he did little to exploit their exegetical potential as a route into the mind of the canonical editor.

Wilson's work prompted a wave of new Psalm studies. J. Clinton McCann's collection of essays *The Shape and Shaping of the Psalter* (1993) gives a glimpse of the enthusiasm of eminent American Alttestamentler for this new approach. It opens with an essay by J. L. Mays and responses from R. E. Murphy and W. Brueggemann. The last suggests the Psalms should be seen "as a dramatic struggle from obedience (Psalm 1) through dismay (Psalm 73 after 72) to praise (Psalm 150)."[18] Wilson contributes two essays to the collection. In the second of these he argues that the Psalter is bound together by two frameworks: the inner framework relates to the Davidic covenant (Psalms 2, 72, 89, 144), whereas the outer is a final wisdom frame (Psalms 1, 73, 90, 107, 145).

Perhaps the most stimulating article in this collection is P. D. Miller's "Beginning of the Psalter," which puts the structural insights of Wilson and others into the service of exegetical theology. Psalms 1 and 2 are often held to come from different redactional layers, though some have argued that the two were originally a single psalm that has been split in two (cf. Psalms 42–43). But whichever diachronic explanation is right, in the present Psalter the two psalms are distinct but closely related verbally and this needs to be borne in mind as we interpret them.

Psalm 1 sets the agenda for the Psalter by dividing mankind into two categories: the righteous, who keep the law and inherit God's blessing, and the wicked, who suffer destruction. These two groups of people keep on reappearing in the subsequent psalms. In the laments the righteous repeatedly cry out to God for deliverance from their oppressors, the wicked. Miller explains that in "Psalm 37, we have the most extensive discourse on the relation of the wicked and the righteous and their two ways outside of Psalm 1. In general, the plight of the victim, the *tsaddiq*, in the face of the

---

[18] J. Clinton McCann Jr., *The Shape and Shaping of the Psalter* (Sheffield: Sheffield Academic Press, 2000), 41.

wicked is very much to the fore at the beginning of the Psalter and throughout much of Book 1."[19]

Also prominent in Psalm 1 is the joy of studying the Torah, and its positive benefits for those who do. This emphasis on obeying the law reappears elsewhere in book 1 of the Psalter. Psalms 15 and 24 are entrance liturgies setting out the moral requirements for those who would worship in the temple, while Psalm 19 compares the life-giving power of the Torah to that of the sun. The penultimate psalm of book 1 echoes the sentiments of Psalm 1:

> I *delight* to do your will, O my God;
>> your *law* is within my heart. (Ps. 40:8)

After Psalm 1 comes Psalm 2, which sounds another note. It is all about the king and the nations and their rulers who plan to attack him. This theme of the king under attack is explicit in the next three royal psalms, 18, 20, 21. But the juxtaposition of Psalms 1 and 2 suggests that the righteous of Psalm 1 could be identified with the king of Psalm 2, while the wicked of Psalm 1 could be the king's enemies. This seems to be confirmed by comparing 1:6, "the way of the wicked will perish," with the warning to the king's enemies in 2:12,

> Kiss the Son,
>> lest he be angry, and you perish in the way.

This linkage between the two psalms leads to two insights into how the subsequent psalms in book 1 should be read. The first, says Miller, is "that we are to hear in the psalms the voice of the king, however subtly it may be present."[20] This suggestion is reinforced by the psalm titles of book 1, which all include an ascription to David. Thus Psalm 3 "is understood easily, if not preferably, as

---

[19] P. D. Miller, "The Beginning of the Psalter," in ibid., 85–86.
[20] Ibid., 88.

the voice of the king surrounded by his foes and praying for God's deliverance and blessing on the people or nation."[21]

On first sight Psalm 8 does not fit this observation, though it does mention foes in verse 3. It is, though, thoroughly integrated into the sequence of psalms: it focuses on the majesty of God's name (vv. 1, 9), which is how Psalm 7 closes and Psalm 9 begins (see 7:17; 9:2).

Second, echoing Genesis 1:26–28 it teaches that every human being is a king.

> What is man that you are mindful of him,
>   and the son of man that you care for him?
>
> Yet you have . . .
>   crowned him with glory and honor.
> You have given him dominion over the works of your hands;
>   you have put all things under his feet. (Ps. 8:4–6)

This allows us to see the righteous sufferer as not only a just king who upholds the law, but any righteous person who does this. Miller explains:

> While Psalm 2 invites the reader to hear the voice of the Lord's anointed in the following psalms, Psalm 1 says that what we hear is the voice of *anyone* who lives by the Torah, which may and should include the king. But as such, the anointed one is simply a true Israelite, even as he is a true king.[22]

Whybray, *Reading the Psalms as a Book*

The first British contribution to this debate came from R. N. Whybray, well known for his studies of the Wisdom Literature. In *Reading the Psalms as a Book* he examines the claims that the Psalter has been systematically arranged to bring out the two main themes of obedience to the law and the promises to David.

---

[21] Ibid.
[22] Ibid., 91–92.

Whybray is somewhat skeptical about the first, but more positive toward the second. He acknowledges that a number of wisdom psalms stress that obedience to the law will be rewarded, and that several of them open different books of the Psalter (Psalm 1, book 1; Psalm 73, book 3; Psalm 90, book 4; and Psalm 107, book 5). He also allows that quite a few psalms seem to have been tweaked editorially to give them a wisdom thrust (e.g., Pss. 18:20–24;[23] 92:5–9, 12–14).[24] He suggests that Psalm 19 originally consisted only of verses 1–6 (about the sun) and that the rest of the psalm (vv. 7–14, about the law) was added later by a wisdom editor.[25]

But this, according to Whybray, does not add up to prove that the book of Psalms has undergone a systematic wisdom redaction. He is very dubious about the claim of Howard and others that there are verbal linkages between consecutive psalms. Whybray suspects these apparent links may be in the mind of the reader rather than the editor of the Psalter.[26] He does not dismiss those who see some loose progression in the Psalter—e.g., from obedience to praise—but his main concern is not to read too much into the development. He finds "no tangible evidence of a consistent and systematic attempt to link the whole collection together by editorial means."[27]

Whybray is more impressed by the positioning of the royal psalms 2, 72, and 89 at the seams of the books. He is favorably inclined to seeing the position of these psalms as pointing to an eschatological or messianic reading, though he does not find much evidence of redactional modification to these psalms to make this clearer. Psalm 2, for example, envisages a universal rule for the Davidic king, something neither he nor any of his successors achieved. In the postexilic era when there was no Israelite king at all, the psalm could have been understood to express a hope

---

[23] R. Norman Whybray, *Reading the Psalms as a Book*, JSOTSup 222 (Sheffield: Sheffield Academic Press, 1996), 51.

[24] Ibid., 55.

[25] Ibid., 46.

[26] Ibid., 81–83.

[27] Ibid., 84.

for a new David. In such a situation "a messianic interpretation would be a natural one."[28] Whybray thinks the last verses of Psalm 18 might also point in this direction, and especially verses 7–15, which picture God appearing in a Sinai-style theophany to help the king. It is natural to take them as "speaking of a 'new David' greater than the historical David."[29] Whybray thinks that Psalm 72 envisages not simply the Davidic dynasty lasting forever, as 2 Samuel 7 promises, but the particular king reigning forever (Ps. 72:5). "The hyperbolic language" points "beyond the present to a future saviour-figure."[30]

While Wilson and McCann argue that Psalm 89 suggests that the failure of the promises to David prepares the way for book 4 of the Psalter, which celebrates the reign of Yahweh substituting for the rule of David's son, Whybray disagrees. He reads verse 46, "How long, O LORD? Will you hide yourself forever?" and verse 49, "Lord, where is your steadfast love of old?" as cries not of despair but of faith.

> It is important to bear in mind that laments in the Psalter . . . are not expressions of despair. However much the psalmists may accuse God of breaking his word and becoming an enemy, hope always remains that intercession will be effective: hence the characteristic "How long?" . . . Even in apparently hopeless circumstances . . . the psalmists continued to hope. So here in Psalm 89 the psalmist urges God not to forget the promises that he has made that the Davidic dynasty would be forever (vv. 5, 22, 29, 30) and stresses his faithfulness in passages to which he gives such prominence that they cannot have been intended merely as foils for the account which follows of disillusion and consequent loss of faith.[31]

Whybray argues that the very positive remarks about the Davidic king in book 5, especially Psalms 110 and 132, also make

[28] Ibid., 90.
[29] Ibid., 91.
[30] Ibid., 92.
[31] Ibid., 93–94.

it hard to believe that the compilers of the Psalter had lost hope in the revival of the Davidic dynasty.[32]

Jean-Marie Auwers also holds that the editors of the Psalter believed that the promises to David were still valid, but he is unsure whether this involves a restoration of the Davidic monarchy, a personal messiah, or a collective messianism. "So, when Israel recites the psalms, it does it *in persona David*, and YHWH recognises the voice of the son of Jesse through that of the faithful. The sap of the Jesse tree still flows in their veins."[33]

The Titles

Final-form and canonical readings of the Psalter have to take seriously the psalm titles. Traditional critics disregarded these titles, holding that they were nearly all later accretions that, despite their claims, tell us very little about authorship or the contexts in which the psalms originated. Most canonical critics would not dispute that the titles give no historical information about the psalms' origins, but it is clear that these titles were important for the Psalter's editors, who either knew the psalms with their titles or added the titles themselves. Either way the titles give an important glimpse into the way the psalms were interpreted. The grouping of psalms by author (David, Asaph, etc.) or type (Songs of Ascents) probably reflects the contents of earlier psalm collections from which the present Psalter was compiled. But in the present setting in the canonical Psalter, that is not the function of the titles: they encourage the reader to understand a psalm with a particular heading in a particular way.

The Psalter contains several groups of psalms with the title "A Psalm of David." The first of these, the first Davidic Psalter, consists of Psalms 3–41. Psalm 3 is headed "A Psalm of David, when he fled from Absalom his son." But this is not the first time David's voice is heard in the Psalter: he is clearly the main speaker in Psalm 2, where he introduces himself as the Lord's anointed.

---

[32] Ibid., 94–98.
[33] Auwers, *La composition littéraire du psautier*, 122 (my trans.).

But the key-word linkages between each psalm and the next, as well as the Davidic titles, create the impression that the prayer continues through the psalms without interruption, putting the whole collection under the patronage of David.[34]

Furthermore, when the titles with biographical elements as in Psalms 3, 7, 18, 34, 51, 52, 54, 56, 57, 59, 60, 63, 142 are analyzed, it appears that most of them relate to the period before David became king and describe his persecution by Saul. Of the three that are placed in David's reign (Psalms 3, 51, 60), the first two describe unhappy episodes, his flight from Absalom (3) and his adultery with Bathsheba (51).

> The "historical" titles of the Psalter thus depict . . . a David not yet established, whose tears and wandering steps are reckoned in the great divine book (Ps. 56:9). This David is shaped according to the image of his poor people and so becomes a model for Israel in his humiliation and wanderings. The historical titles thus give to the reader of the psalms as a type and model, a certain David, full of humility, trust in YHWH, and penitence. Paradoxically the attribution of the Psalter to David has the effect of facilitating the appropriation of the psalms by every pious Israelite, in so far as the son of Jesse has been presented as the model with which each one ought to seek to identify himself.[35]

The theological significance of the Davidic titles has been more fully explored by Martin Kleer in *Der liebliche Sänger der Psalmen Israels* (1996). Kleer holds that the phrase *leDawid* originally meant "about David" and that at a later stage in transmission, when the biographical elements were being included, it came to be understood as indicating authorship "by David."[36] This makes book 1 of the Psalter a spiritual diary of the praying David.

> With the help of his psalms David goes on his way from distress to salvation, from the depths to the heights, not without

---

[34] Ibid., 136.
[35] Ibid., 151 (my trans.).
[36] Martin Kleer, *Der liebliche Sänger der Psalmen Israels* (Bodenheim: Philo, 1996), 78–85.

many heights and depths on the way, until he can finally confess, "Blessed be the LORD, the God of Israel, from everlasting to everlasting! Amen and Amen" (Psalm 41:13). The first Davidic Psalter thus invites those who pray, especially the poor and needy, to accompany and follow this spiritual path with and like David, through praying his psalms.[37]

Most of the biographical headings are found in the second Davidic collection, which runs from Psalms 51 to 72. Kleer notes that these biographical snippets draw not on the portrait of David found in Chronicles, where he is portrayed as the founder of the temple and the organizer of its worship, but on the difficult periods in his life mentioned in the books of Samuel, not in Chronicles. "The biographical headings portray David predominantly as the persecuted, betrayed and captured, as the mourning and guilty one."[38] These psalms exemplify problems that the pious person may experience, and they invite him "like David to overcome . . . particularly life's crises with the help of his psalms and with God."[39]

Book 2 concludes with Psalm 72, whose title "to" or "by Solomon" ("Of Solomon," ESV) leads Kleer to take this Psalm as a prayer by David for Solomon. Thus the first two Davidic collections cover episodes from David's life, though not in chronological order. But the great hopes for David's descendants expressed in Psalm 72 were apparently shattered by the fall of Jerusalem and the monarchy, events alluded to in many psalms of book 3, most explicitly in the final one, Psalm 89.

However, books 4 and 5 respond to the lament of Psalm 89 with the call to trust in the Lord's rule, not in human rulers, "without giving up the hope in the eternity of the Davidic covenant."[40] Kleer holds that in the fourth and fifth books of the Psalter, the Davidic psalms must be understood as the psalms of a future

---

[37] Ibid., 93 (my trans.).
[38] Ibid., 116 (my trans.).
[39] Ibid., 118 (my trans.).
[40] Ibid., 120 (my trans.).

David. For example, Psalms 101–4 do not look backward but forward. Psalm 101 envisages a new Davidic king, whose prayer (102) will lead to the universal recognition of Yahweh (Psalms 102–3).

In the fifth book of the Psalms are two Davidic collections (Psalms 108–10) and (Psalms 138–45), placed at both ends of the book. In Psalm 110 Yahweh is given victory over those who were afflicting the new David in Psalms 108–9. Despite oppression, this David maintains his faith in the Lord and praises him before the nations, so the Lord "installs the new David as royal-priestly Messiah and intervenes himself against the enemies."[41] The second Davidic collection (Psalms 138–45) is the new David's response to the questions and doubts of the exiles (Ps. 137:4). For Psalm 138 this is an opportunity to make the praise of the Lord clear to all the kings of the earth (138:4), while the last verse of Psalm 145 announces the theme of the concluding Hallel (Psalms 146–50), "let all flesh bless his holy name forever and ever" (Ps. 145:21).

Hossfeld and Zenger's Commentary

Kleer's study is one of a number[42] that give an overview of how the Psalms may be read canonically. There is an inevitable tendency in such works to focus on the points that can be easily connected and to ignore psalms or parts of psalms that do not fit into the pattern. But a commentator must not do this: he must exegete every verse, and this poses challenges for canonical reading. These challenges are tackled head on by Hossfeld and Zenger in their contribution to Herders Theologischer Kommentar zum Alten Testament. It therefore seems fitting to summarize their treatment of a particular psalm to illustrate canonical exegesis in practice. Their volume deals with only a third of the Psalter, so there is much work yet to be done.

Zenger summed up his principles of canonical exegesis of the

---

[41] Ibid., 123 (my trans.).

[42] E.g., David M. Howard, *The Structure of Psalms 93–100* (Winona Lake, IN: Eisenbrauns, 1997); David C. Mitchell, *The Message of the Psalter: An Eschatological Programme in the Book of Psalms* (Sheffield: Sheffield Academic Press, 1997); and R. L. Cole, *The Shape and Message of Book 3 (Psalms 73–89)* (Sheffield: Sheffield Academic Press, 2000).

Psalms in an article entitled "What Is Different about Canonical Exegesis of the Psalms?," published in 1991.[43]

1. Canonical exegesis pays attention to the connections between one psalm and its neighbors.
2. Canonical exegesis pays attention to the position of a psalm within its redactional unit.
3. Canonical exegesis sees the titles of the psalms as an interpretative horizon.
4. Canonical exegesis takes into consideration the connections and repetitions of psalms within the collection.

Before examining how these principles operate in the interpretation of a particular psalm, we should say something about Hossfeld and Zenger's diachronic assumptions. For they are not content with a final-form synchronic exegesis, but frequently use the presumed origin of a psalm or its place in an earlier collection to illuminate the meaning of the text.

The earliest (pre-exilic) collection of psalms is found in Psalms 3–41. In the exile various subcollections were assembled, which were brought together in a final redaction of the Psalter between 200 and 150 BC.

Within these later collections, Psalms 52–68, which are full of war imagery, were probably brought together first. In the fifth century this exilic collection was expanded and given a Davidic coloring to produce the second Davidic Psalter, Psalms 51–72. Also in the fifth century this Davidic Psalter was expanded by encircling it with the psalms of Asaph (Psalms 50, 73–83) and prefacing it with the psalms of the sons of Korah (Psalms 42–49). Still in the Persian period, further psalms were added at the beginning (Psalm 2) and end of the collection (Psalm 89) to create a messianic Psalter. It was in this phase that the first three books were distinguished in that each ended with a doxology (Ps. 41:13; 72:18–19; 89:52).

Psalms 90–92, a tightly integrated group, are the first response

---

[43] Erich Zenger, "Was wird anders bei kanonischer Psalmenauslegung?," in *Ein Gott*, ed. Friedrich V. Reiterer (Würzburg: Echter Verlag, 1991).

to the issues raised by the messianic Psalter. Psalms 93–100, "the LORD is king" psalms forming another clear group, concluded a fourth-century version of the whole Psalter, which then consisted of Psalms 2–100.[44]

For an example of Hossfeld and Zenger's canonical interpretation, we shall look at Psalm 51, the greatest of the penitential psalms, also known as *Miserere mei*. After a bibliography and translation the commentary begins with detailed notes on the text and translation. These emphasize syntactical issues and show an aversion to emending the Masoretic Text. Under the heading "Analysis" there follows a fairly conventional discussion of the genre of the psalm (penitential), a discussion of its sections, and the case for seeing verses 18–19 as an addition to the original psalm (vv. 1–17), which was composed in the postexilic era.

It is under *Auslegung* ("Exposition") that some of the characteristics of canonical exegesis start to be apparent. It begins with a long discussion of the title, which ascribes the psalm to David and connects it with his affair with Bathsheba. Zenger notes that this is the first of a series of biographical notes connecting psalms with episodes in David's life, mostly from the time of his conflict with Saul. These make a theological point that David suffered as a result of his affair, and his prayer for forgiveness (51:1–12) is not really answered until 65:2:

> O you who hear prayer,
>   to you shall all flesh come.

Despite the praise that follows (Psalms 65–68), David still suffers for God's sake (Psalm 69). David does not see true *shalom* himself, but Solomon his son does (72:3, 7). "What began with David's crime against Bathsheba ends at last with the peaceful reign of Solomon, the son of David and Bathsheba. David's sin was transformed into the salvation that Solomon was permitted to experience."[45]

---

[44] Frank-Lothar Hossfeld and Erich Zenger, *Psalms 2: A Commentary on Psalms 51–100*, trans. Linda M. Maloney (Minneapolis: Augsburg, 2005), 1–7.

[45] Ibid., 19, quoting Kleer, *Der liebliche Sänger der Psalmen Israels*, 111–12.

Then follows a full and thorough discussion of the theology of 51:1–17, with much cross-referencing to the Pentateuch and other psalms. Notably absent though is discussion of 2 Samuel 11–12 and its possible relationship to this psalm. In other words the exegesis is on the original psalm in its posited postexilic original setting. Psalm 51:18–19 with its prayer that God will build up the walls of Jerusalem is not speaking about a literal rebuilding of Jerusalem such as Nehemiah carried out—for according to Zenger these verses postdate Nehemiah—but it is praying about the eschatological renewal of Jerusalem. This renewal is something that the postexilic theology, especially the Isaianic school, used to dream of.[46] In this revived city, whose inhabitants have been saved by God from their guilt and have experienced re-creation, their sacrifices will be acceptable to God. Though these last two verses were added later to the psalm, Zenger thinks they make a very fitting conclusion.

> The people who have been newly created through the forgiveness of their sin are in reality the ideal inhabitants of the new Jerusalem. Conversely the renewal of Zion as the centre of creation begins with the re-creation of its inhabitants. Indeed where sinners allow themselves to be re-created by YHWH, the people of God will be renewed. And when this occurs on Zion . . . Jerusalem will be the city of righteousness.[47]

Under "Context. Reception, Meaning" Zenger explores subsequent settings and interpretations of the psalm. First is the stage of its incorporation into the second Davidic Psalter (Psalms 51–72). At this stage the title was added and the psalm became seen as David's confession. Zenger notes many verbal affinities in Psalm 51 with the accounts in 2 Samuel 11–12. The deliberate positioning of the psalm as the first in this collection gives it a programmatic quality, making David a model for Israel, even a mes-

---

[46] Hossfeld and Zenger, *Psalms 2*, 22–23.
[47] Frank-Lothar Hossfeld and Erich Zenger, *Die Psalmen II: Psalm 51–100* (Freiburg: Herder, 2002), 56 (my trans.). Cf. *Psalms 2*, trans. Maloney, 23.

sianic figure. "From David Israel should learn that whoever stands can fall, but also whoever has fallen can by the mercy of God . . . be raised up again, even be re-created."[48]

But Psalm 51 serves not only as a programmatic opening to the second Davidic Psalter, but also as a summary of the end of the first Davidic Psalter, Psalms 35–41. Even closer connections may be seen between Psalms 50 and 51. Both criticize empty sacrificial ritual and demand worship that springs from an acknowledgment of one's helplessness and from a righteous lifestyle (50:8–15; cf. 51:14–19). They are also linked by the theme of God's judging and saving righteousness (50:6 [cf. 51:4, 14]; 50:23 [cf. 51:12, 14]).[49] This link between Psalms 50 and 51 ties together the second Davidic Psalter (Psalms 51–72) with the Asaph collection (Psalms 50, 73–83). The Asaph collection engages with the theological crisis engendered by the destruction of the temple. Both psalms present a critique of worthless sacrifice and a vision of sacrificial worship that is acceptable to God. At the same time the promise of a rebuilding of Jerusalem by Yahweh (Ps. 51:18) gives the laments in the Asaph collection about the destruction of the temple and the city a special piquancy.

Zenger does not explicitly discuss the meaning of the psalm within the context of the complete Psalter, though obviously his comments on the Davidic theme of the Psalter give some pointers in that direction. He then makes a few comments on the way the Septuagint and Targum translate the psalm, before offering some reflections on the New Testament use of Psalm 51. In Jesus's parables of the prodigal son and the Pharisee and the publican, both penitents quote Psalm 51:1, 4 (cf. Luke 18:13; 15:18, 21). More importantly Luke 15 gives a vivid illustration of the whole structure of Psalm 51: acknowledgment of sin, confession to a merciful God, re-creation, festive meal.

Though Paul quotes Psalm 51 only in Romans 3:4, Zenger holds that the psalm forms the background to the whole of Paul's

---

[48] Hossfeld and Zenger, *Die Psalmen II*, 56 (my trans.). Cf. *Psalms 2*, trans. Maloney, 23.

[49] Hossfeld and Zenger, *Psalms 2*, 24.

discussion in Romans 1:18–3:31, which concerns the revelation of God's wrath on those who reject the knowledge of God, and the eschatological revealing of God's saving righteousness.[50]

This discussion of the New Testament use of Psalm 51 paves the way for Zenger's final section, *Bedeutung* ("Significance"), where he reflects on the subsequent use of the psalm. It is important in the Jewish Day of Atonement liturgy and is the Christian penitential psalm *par excellence*. It paved the way for Luther's doctrine of grace. Though some have misapplied 51:5 to prove the doctrine of original sin, the psalm does bear witness to the environment of guilt into which everyone is born and which everyone perpetuates by his own sin. "But at the same time the psalm insists that the destructiveness of this context of sin is countered by the renewing, life-giving concern of the merciful God."[51]

Summary

This chapter has sought to trace the development of canonical readings of the Psalms: from Childs—via Wilson, Whybray, and Kleer—to Hossfeld and Zenger. Many others have contributed to the discussion, but space does not permit further discussion. I hope my selection gives a glimpse of the best of canonical readings of the Psalms.

There is I think no doubt that this approach has led to a deeper and richer theological reading of the Psalms, one that is especially congenial to the Christian interpreter. The earlier historically orientated and form-critical readings seem threadbare by comparison. But this is not to say that any of the studies included here are the last word on the subject. There are a number of issues that need further discussion.

The most fundamental question is, What is the canonical context in which we read each psalm? Hossfeld and Zenger see a variety of contexts for reading each psalm. They look at the meaning of Psalm 51 in its original form (i.e., minus its title and last two

---

[50] Ibid., 24–25.
[51] Ibid., 25.

verses), its meaning as part of the second Davidic Psalter, its setting when linked with the psalms of Asaph, and its use in the New Testament and in Christian and Jewish devotion. McCann,[52] by contrast, focuses on the meaning of Psalm 51 in the present book of the Psalms with some reference to the New Testament. Now which of these contexts is most appropriate for a canonical reading, or are all equally valid?

I tend to think three canonical contexts are more important than others. First, there is the canonical context of the whole Psalter. If, as I think has been demonstrated, the psalms have been arranged thematically, by title, and by key words to form a deliberate sequence, it is imperative to read one psalm in the context of the whole collection and, in particular, in relationship to its near neighbors.

The second important context is reading the Psalms in the context of the Jewish canon, the Hebrew Bible. The various psalms themselves invite this by their frequent reference to historical figures and episodes from the past. Some, such as 104–6, seem to retell the Pentateuch in poetic fashion. Psalm 1 invites the reader to meditate on the law day and night. The titles of the psalms, as well as some of the texts, point to David's connection with the psalms. Furthermore in writing Old Testament theology it is surely appropriate to compare the message of the Psalms with other works, such as Chronicles, that originated in the postexilic era.

Third, of course, the Psalms need to be read in the context of the Christian canon of the Old and New Testaments. The Psalms are the book of the Old Testament most quoted in the New: it appears that the early Christians inhabited the thought world of the Psalms, so that any biblical theology that would be Christian must read the Psalms in this context.[53]

The second major issue facing the canonical reader is not simply knowing which literary context to read the text in, but also

[52] J. Clinton McCann Jr., "The Book of the Psalms," in *The New Interpreter's Bible*, vol. 4, ed. Leander E. Keck et al. (Nashville: Abingdon, 1996), 884–89.
[53] Steve Moyise and Maarten J. Menken, eds., *The Psalms in the New Testament* (London: T&T Clark, 2004).

which historical setting. Should we see the Psalter as compiled during the exile, after the exile, or even later? It could make a difference to the way we read it. Wilson[54] appears to favor the final arrangement of the Psalter in the first century AD, Hossfeld and Zenger[55] say early in the second century BC, and Auwers[56] thinks somewhere between 350 BC and 200 BC is possible. McCann,[57] on the other hand, does not think it really matters, since we know little about the postexilic era, and throughout it the Jews did not enjoy independence, monarchical rule, or real ownership of the land. These deficits were grave drawbacks, especially when contrasted with the hopes and aspirations expressed in the Psalms. We could therefore read the psalms as reassertions of these historic beliefs in the face of present experience.

A similar uncertainty surrounds the place of the Psalms within the Hebrew canon, for we cannot be sure when that was closed. At least that problem does not arise with the Christian canon, for from the beginning of the Christian era the Psalms formed part of Christian devotion. But should a Christian canonical reading be based in the first century AD, or are other later settings just as valid as canonical readings?

Finally, we must admit the tentativeness of canonical readings offered to date. There are plenty of divergent interpretations offered by those who believe in reading the Psalter in its final form. Many issues require further discussion. And there are still those who hold that there is no method underlying the arrangement of the Psalter—that it is all eisegesis. This chapter presupposes that such skepticism is unwarranted, but I have also drawn attention to unanswered questions that canonical approaches raise. How does the wisdom theme cohere with the royal theme? Is a messianic reading of books 4 and 5 of the Psalter justified? How far can one go with the early church in reading the Psalms as prophecy?

---

[54] Wilson, *The Editing of the Hebrew Psalter*, 92. This is much too late because the Septuagint translation of the Psalter dates from about 200 BC; so Auwers, *La composition littéraire du psautier*, 168.
[55] Hossfeld and Zenger, *Psalms 2*, 27.
[56] Auwers, *La composition littéraire du psautier*, 170.
[57] McCann, "The Book of the Psalms," 661.

The voice of the righteous royal figure who suffers persecution is often heard in the Psalms and clearly invites christological interpretation. But we must ask if this is warranted.[58] Much attention has been paid to the Davidic titles and their significance in interpretation, but what about the titles ascribing psalms to Asaph or the sons of Korah? Should we see them as more than just telling us about their source? Diachronic issues must also not be forgotten: for example, the dating of individual psalms. Are any of the titles authentic?[59] And if they are, does that make a difference to interpretation? These are just some of the issues that need further discussion in years to come. But they are relatively minor. They should not obscure the great gains canonical reading of the Psalms has brought us. To quote Brevard Childs:

> The canonical shape of the Psalter assured the future generations of Israelites that this book spoke a word of God to each of them in their need. It was not only a record of the past, but a living voice speaking to the present human suffering. By taking seriously the canonical shape the reader is given an invaluable resource for the care of souls, as the synagogue and church have always understood the Psalter to be.[60]

---

[58] For an argument in favor, see G. Braulik, "Psalter and Messiah: Towards a Christological Understanding of the Psalms in the Old Testament and the Church Fathers," in *Psalms and Liturgy*, ed. D. J. Human and C. J. A. Vos (London: T&T Clark, 2004), 15–40.

[59] Michael D. Goulder, *The Prayers of David (Psalms 51–72)* (Sheffield: JSOT Press, 1990), 24, argues that these psalms do originate in the Davidic era, perhaps written by a son of David "for David."

[60] Brevard S. Childs, *Introduction to the Old Testament as Scripture* (London: SCM, 1979), 523.

Chapter 4

Reading the Psalms Messianically[1]

At Christmas time it is customary in many towns for the local choral society to put on a performance of Handel's *Messiah*. It is often also broadcast on national radio at this time of year. Most people know the great "Hallelujah" chorus, concluding part 2, in which everyone in the audience is supposed to stand. Just before this there is a series of bass and tenor arias and a chorus, all drawn from Psalm 2.

The bass sings:

> Why do the nations so furiously rage together? and why do the people imagine a vain thing?
> The kings of the earth rise up, and the rulers take counsel together against the Lord, and against His Anointed. (Ps. 2:1–2)

The chorus responds,

> Let us break their bonds asunder, and cast away their yokes from us. (Ps. 2:3)

Finally the tenor comments:

> He that dwelleth in heaven shall laugh them to scorn; the Lord shall have them in derision.
> Thou shalt break them with a rod of iron; Thou shalt dash them in pieces like a potter's vessel. (Ps. 2:4, 9)

---

[1] A lecture given at The Southern Baptist Theological Seminary, March 27, 2006; not previously published.

Handel, or more precisely his librettist, Charles Jennens, like nearly all Christians and Jews in the preceding two millennia, clearly assumed that Psalm 2 is prophetic, proclaiming the reign of God's Son, the Messiah, at the end of time. That is the view I unconsciously imbibed in my youth as every Christmas we listened to the *Messiah* on the radio.

Imagine then my shock and consternation when, as a freshman attending the only good first-year course on the Old Testament at the University of Cambridge, I was told that Psalm 2 and the other psalms traditionally held to be messianic were not that at all: they were about the king in Jerusalem. Psalm 2, it was asserted, was used at the coronation of Davidic kings in Jerusalem. It should not be read prophetically at all. This was one of the "assured results" of criticism!

It is my purpose in this chapter to question this "assured" result. My previous chapter on reading the Psalms canonically has already touched on this issue. For devotees of canonical criticism it is a bit passé to deny the messianic interpretation of these psalms, but not everyone is a canonical critic just yet; many are still mired in form and historical criticism. So I thought in this chapter that it would be worthwhile to take a closer look at the issue. Particularly, I want to examine which psalms should be called messianic, how the New Testament reads them, and how the practice of canonical reading contributes to resolving the issue. But before we do this, I think it is useful to review briefly the history of the interpretation of the messianic psalms. This I hope will prevent us just being victims of the current fads in scholarship. So I shall look first at the main trends in psalm interpretation before the rise of modern criticism, and then explain how modern scholars came to deny the messianic sense of the psalms.

The History of Interpretation

We begin a review in pre-Christian times. The book of the prophet Zechariah (9:10) quotes Psalm 72:8:

> May he have dominion from sea to sea,
>> and from the River to the ends of the earth!

Zechariah 9:10 says,

> I will cut off the chariot from Ephraim
>> and the war horse from Jerusalem;
> and the battle bow shall be cut off,
>> and he shall speak peace to the nations;
> his rule shall be from sea to sea,
>> and from the River to the ends of the earth.

The date of the last few chapters of Zechariah is uncertain;[2] they could come from the early fifth century BC and be roughly contemporary with the period in which the psalms were being gathered into a book. But whatever the exact date of Zechariah and the editing of the psalms, this quotation clearly shows that messianic interpretation of some psalms occurred long before the Christian era, because Zechariah is clearly prophesying a future ruler, not commenting on a past one.

The early Jewish translations of the Psalms into Greek and Aramaic indicate that Jews understood the Psalms messianically too. Again, the date of these translations is a matter of some conjecture, but the Septuagint of Psalms may date from the early second century BC, and the Targum and Syriac a few centuries later. For example the Targum paraphrases Psalm 21:1 as "King Messiah shall rejoice in your strength, O Lord," and the Syriac heads Psalm 72 with the title "A Psalm of David, when he had made Solomon king, and a prophecy concerning the advent of the Messiah and the calling of the Gentiles."[3]

The New Testament, of course, takes many of the psalms as predicting the life of Christ, and to this we shall return later. But, interestingly, it also implies that some of Jesus's opponents also

---

[2] See Rex Mason, *The Books of Haggai, Zechariah, and Malachi* (Cambridge: Cambridge University Press, 1977), 77–79.

[3] For further discussion, see David C. Mitchell, *The Message of the Psalter: An Eschatological Programme in the Book of Psalms* (Sheffield: Sheffield Academic Press), 18–21.

read the Psalms messianically. For instance, in Matthew 22:41–46 and its parallels,[4] says David Mitchell, "the Pharisees are depicted as tacitly accepting the Davidic authorship of Psalm 110, even though Davidic authorship is the very point on which the Christian apologia depends."[5] Other books of the New Testament that appeal to the psalms to demonstrate Christian positions include Acts, Hebrews, and John's Gospel. "So if then," Mitchell reasons, "early Christian Israelites (Messianic Jews) employed Psalms as messianic proof-texts, it follows that their opponents must have acknowledged the messianic referent of these same texts."[6]

The rightness of this conclusion is demonstrated by the way that in the succeeding centuries both Jews and Christians continued to interpret the Psalms messianically. Let me note just a few Christian examples. In the second century Justin Martyr "cites Psalms 2, 3, 22, 24, 68, 72 and 110 as messianic proof-texts."[7] Athanasius in the fourth century affirms, "When we come to the matters of which the Prophets speak we find that these occur in almost all. Of the coming of the Saviour and how, although He is God, He yet should dwell among us, Psalm 50 says: 'God shall come openly, even our God.'"[8] Athanasius adds, "Having shown that Christ should come in human form, the Psalter goes on to show that He can suffer in the flesh He has assumed."[9] He then continues with quotes from Psalms 2, 22, 88, 69, 138, and 72. He finds the ascension proclaimed in Psalms 24, 47, 110, the final judgment in 9, 72, 50, and 82, and the calling of the Gentiles in 47 and 72.[10] St. Augustine in the fifth century also finds messianic prophecies throughout the Psalter. For example at the beginning of his commentary on Psalm 3 he says,

---

[4] Mark 12:35–37; Luke 20:41–44.
[5] Mitchell, *The Message of the Psalter*, 27.
[6] Ibid., 28.
[7] Ibid., 36.
[8] Athanasius, *On the Incarnation*, with appendix "On the Interpretation of the Psalms," ed. and trans. a religious of C.S.M.V. (New York: St Vladimir's Seminary Press, 1977), 99.
[9] Ibid., 100.
[10] Ibid., 101–2.

The words, "I slept, and took rest; and rose, for the Lord will take me up," lead us to believe that this Psalm is to be understood as in the Person of Christ; for they sound more applicable to the Passion and Resurrection of our Lord, than to that history in which David's flight is described from the face of his rebellious son.[11]

The great Reformers continued this prophetic approach to Psalm interpretation. Luther commented, "For this reason alone the Psalter should be precious and beloved: because it promises Christ's death and resurrection clearly and depicts his kingdom and the entire condition and nature of Christendom."[12] Luther sees the different collections of psalms focusing on different aspects of our Lord's career. The sons of Korah speak of the incarnation, while the psalms of David speak more of the passion and resurrection.[13] Calvin and Bucer likewise see the Psalms as referring both to the historical David and to the future David, the Christ.

But in the nineteenth century this way of reading the Psalms went into retreat. Some leading traditionalists maintained that the Psalms had a messianic sense, notably Hengstenberg and Delitzsch[14] in Germany and Alexander at Princeton, but the tide of scholarship was flowing against them. Deism in England and the Enlightenment on the Continent had a profound effect on the development of biblical criticism. At its heart, though not always expressed, was a deep antipathy to the supernatural and the principle of revelation: hence an approach to the Psalms that saw them as prophesying the coming of Christ was quite incompatible with the fundamental ideas of the Enlightenment. Furthermore, in the wake of Descartes, it was held that everything had to be proved from scratch, rather than accepted on the basis of authority.

[11] Augustine, *Enarrationes in psalmos* 3.1 (trans. J. E. Tweed, *NPNF*[1], vol. 8).

[12] Luther, *Psalmen-Auslegung* (ed. E. Mühlhaupt, 1965) 1.3, quoted in Mitchell, *The Message of the Psalter*, 39.

[13] Mitchell, *The Message of the Psalter*, 39n104.

[14] Cf. Franz Delitzsch, *Biblical Commentary on the Psalms* (1871; repr., Grand Rapids: Eerdmans, n.d.), 1:90, on Psalm 2: "We should at least know the Psalm was composed by a king filled with a lofty Messianic consciousness."

Instead of theology being defined as faith seeking understanding, it became understanding seeking faith. Or to put it more crudely: if you cannot understand it, you cannot accept it.

In New Testament studies this led to all sorts of skepticism about the Gospels and their record of Jesus's life, while many of the epistles were pronounced pseudonymous, a posh word for forgeries. The same happened to the Pentateuch: the books of Moses were no longer Mosaic, but an amalgamation of late sources whose value for reconstructing biblical history was very dubious. The Psalms in their turn suffered from this skepticism. It was not expressed in an overtly theological way, but it had a profound effect on the interpretation of the Psalms.

The main assault on the Psalms took the form of discarding the titles. It was argued that the titles were later additions to the text and were therefore worthless as a guide to the authorship of psalms or their content. At a stroke they were no longer the psalms of David or Asaph or the sons of Korah, dating from the time of the early monarchy—i.e., tenth century BC—but anonymous compositions mostly from the postexilic era down to the Maccabean era, roughly 500 to 150 BC. By writing off the titles in this way, skeptics eliminated the clearest marks of order in the Psalter. In the Psalms' final form the sequence of titles does point to careful arrangement. For example all except one (untitled) psalm in Psalms 3–41 are called psalms of David.

Psalms 73–83 are all psalms of Asaph, while Psalms 120–34 are all "Songs of Ascents." Other signs of careful arrangement such as the division of the Psalter into five books and the concatenation, whereby key words link adjacent psalms, were also ignored.

What then were the arguments that persuaded so many to ignore the psalm titles as a guide to the authorship and the interpretation of the Psalms? S. R. Driver, professor of Hebrew at Oxford, was the most influential propagator of the new critical theories in the English-speaking world at the end of the nineteenth century, so a look at his *Introduction to the Literature of the Old Testament* gives us a glimpse of the arguments deployed to eliminate the psalm titles. He is suspicious that there are so few authors mentioned: just David, the sons of Korah, Asaph, and a couple of others. And why not say who wrote the anonymous psalms? Of the seventy-three psalms assigned to David, Driver feels that many of them are not good enough to be by David. "Many . . . instead of displaying the freshness and originality which we should expect in the founder of Hebrew psalmody, contain frequent conventional phrases."[15] The subjective nature of these arguments is, I think, fairly obvious nowadays.

But Driver has some better arguments, or at least some that require a thoughtful reply. For example, some psalms ascribed to David seem to presuppose the existence of the temple, which was not built in his day. Driver cites Psalm 27:4 as one example.

> One thing have I asked of the LORD,
>   that will I seek after:
> that I may dwell in the house of the LORD
>   all the days of my life,
> to gaze upon the beauty of the LORD
>   and to inquire in his temple.

Driver cannot imagine David praying Psalm 11 on the occasion of Absalom's rebellion.[16] He thinks Psalm 51:18–19 implies a restoration of Jerusalem.

> Do good to Zion in your good pleasure;
>   build up the walls of Jerusalem;
> then will you delight in right sacrifices,
>   in burnt offerings and whole burnt offerings;
>   then bulls will be offered on your altar.

Psalm 22:27–30 presupposes the prophetic teaching of the acceptance of Israel's religion by the nations of the earth.[17]

---

[15] S. R. Driver, *An Introduction to the Literature of the Old Testament* (Edinburgh: T&T Clark, 1894), 352.
[16] Ibid., 353.
[17] Ibid., 355.

All the ends of the earth shall remember
　　and turn to the LORD,
and all the families of the nations
　　shall worship before you.
For kingship belongs to the LORD,
　　and he rules over the nations.

To my mind most of these arguments seem pretty flimsy. Did belief that the nations would honor the God of Israel begin only with the prophets? Psalm 11 does not have a title linking it with Absalom's rebellion: only Psalm 3 does. As for the mention of a temple in David's psalms, we do know that there was a tent shrine where the ark was kept in David's day (2 Sam. 6:17) and that David would have liked to have built a temple (2 Sam. 7:2), so I do not see any difficulty in his composing psalms for use in an early shrine that he saw as a forerunner to his son's temple.

Driver has no real explanation of where the psalm titles came from. But someone must have invented these titles, and that editor, whoever he was, did think that they fit the circumstances of David's life. *And* that editor also lived much closer to David's time than Driver did. So it was a bit rash of nineteenth-century scholars to dismiss these titles quite so cavalierly.

But by the twentieth century this had become critical orthodoxy, and it was a long time before anyone really took the titles seriously. Form criticism was the wave of twentieth-century Psalms studies. Gunkel and his pupil Mowinckel insisted that the proper way to study the psalms was to classify them by types or forms, and then to infer possible settings in which these psalms could have been used. Frequently they posited a setting in the worship of the first temple, the one built by Solomon. Though this was no endorsement of their Davidic origin, it suggested that many of the psalms could have been composed much closer to David's days than nineteenth-century scholars had been inclined to believe. For example, Psalm 110 swung from being a Maccabean-era psalm, c. 150 BC, to being dated in the early monarchy, c. 950 BC.[18]

In particular, Gunkel identified eleven psalms as royal, that is, psalms used on various royal occasions, such as coronations, royal weddings, victory celebrations, and so on. These are Psalms 2, 18, 20, 21, 45, 72, 89, 101, 110, 132, and 144. This classification is based on the explicit mention of the king somewhere in each psalm, and has been widely followed by other scholars.[19] However, some have argued that in many more psalms the voice of the king is to be heard: in other words, the psalm makes better sense if one supposes that the king is speaking, not an ordinary layperson. Using this criterion among others, John Eaton has argued that about half the psalms could be royal.[20] From there it does not seem to me a very big step to suggest that they might be by David!

But even if we stick with Gunkel's short list, we note that it includes some of the most obvious candidates for messianic psalms, namely 2, 45, 72, and 110. However, it does not include psalms such as 22 and 69, which Gunkel and his followers classified as individual laments, that is, prayers of an individual in distress pleading for God's intervention to deliver him. Christians have seen these as prophetic predictions of Christ's passion, a sense excluded by form critics such as Gunkel.

But that is not to say that all form critics deny that the New Testament views these psalms messianically or even that such an interpretation may be a valid rereading of the text. Let me quote from Hans-Joachim Kraus on Psalm 2:

> The NT sees in Jesus Christ God's king who in a comprehensive sense has entered into and fulfilled the rule and office of the OT anointed one. It is significant that both Acts and Revelation cite Psalm 2 in connection with the conflicts between the exalted king Christ and the hostile foreign peoples.[21]

---

[18] For a review, see Leslie C. Allen, *Psalms 101–150* (Waco, TX: Word, 1983), 83–84.

[19] See Philip S. Johnston and David G. Firth, eds., *Interpreting the Psalms: Issues and Approaches* (Leicester: Apollos, 2005), 296–300.

[20] John H. Eaton, *Kingship in the Psalms* (London: SCM, 1976).

[21] Hans-Joachim Kraus, *Psalmen 1–59* (Neukirchen: Neukirchener Verlag, 2003), 155 (my trans).

In the case of Psalm 22 Kraus takes a similar tack. The psalm is not a prophecy of the crucifixion; it is rather a paradigmatic reflection on God-forsakenness. Jesus, by praying this psalm on the cross, "enters into the deepest suffering of God-forsakenness, that those who pray the Old Testament experience . . . that is, Jesus declares his solidarity with the whole fullness of suffering."[22] Kraus admits that this is somewhat less of a connection than the New Testament itself sees between the psalm and the experience of our Lord: the New Testament writers clearly saw the connection as one of prophecy and fulfillment.

In the last two decades canonical criticism and other final-form readings of the text have begun to challenge some of the "assured" critical results of source and form criticism. Canonical criticism, at least as originally proposed by Brevard Childs, does not want to deny the results of historical criticism. In the case of the Psalms this means that the conclusions of the form critics are not rejected when it comes to the original use of the Psalms. Childs would accept that the Psalms were originally written for use in temple worship. He would not argue that the titles of the psalms were as old as the psalms they introduce. But canonical criticism would argue not that messianic interpretation is the invention of the New Testament writers, but that the very arrangement of the Psalter indicates that its editors understood the psalms this way. And canonical criticism does hold that the psalm titles give us an insight into the way psalms were understood by the arrangers of the Psalter. The titles tell us who the editors think wrote which psalm and under what circumstances.

Some Implications of Canonical Reading

In previous chapters I pointed out that the Psalter begins with two introductory psalms, which introduce the twin themes of the book: the blessedness of the righteous (Psalm 1) and the triumph of the son of David, the Son of God (Psalm 2). Psalm 2 is the first

---

[22] Ibid., 333.

of several strategically placed royal psalms that open or close a book of the Psalter. The next is Psalm 72, whose heading is "For [or of] Solomon." Its final verse, "The prayers of David, the son of Jesse, are ended" (v. 20), implies that Psalm 72 is probably a prayer of David for Solomon. Psalm 2:6–8 sets out the divine plan for universal sovereignty.

> "As for me, I have set my King
> on Zion, my holy hill."

> I will tell of the decree:
> The LORD said to me, "You are my Son;
> today I have begotten you.
> Ask of me, and I will make the nations your heritage,
> and the ends of the earth your possession."

Psalm 72 has David praying for the fulfillment of these divine promises:

> May he have dominion from sea to sea,
> and from the River to the ends of the earth!
> May desert tribes bow down before him,
> and his enemies lick the dust!
> May the kings of Tarshish and of the coastlands
> render him tribute;
> may the kings of Sheba and Seba
> bring gifts!
> May all kings fall down before him,
> all nations serve him! (vv. 8–11)

If the Psalter had ended with Psalm 72, we would probably have to agree, reluctantly, with form critics that both psalms were just prayers for a coronation or similar event, and that the exaggerated language about "the ends of the earth" and "all kings falling down before him" were just poetic hyperbole. But the Psalter does not end with Psalm 72; that is only the end of book 2. Book 3 contains a number of gloomy laments, which look as though they may be referring to the destruction of Jerusalem, for example Psalm 74:2–3:

> Remember your congregation, which you have purchased of old,
>   which you have redeemed to be the tribe of your heritage!
>   Remember Mount Zion, where you have dwelt.
> Direct your steps to the perpetual ruins;
>   the enemy has destroyed everything in the sanctuary! (cf.
>   Psalms 79, 83, 88)

But Psalm 89, the last in book 3, is the most explicit. It recalls the promise made to the house of David.

> "Once for all I have sworn by my holiness;
>   I will not lie to David.
> His offspring shall endure forever,
>   his throne as long as the sun before me.
> Like the moon it shall be established forever,
>   a faithful witness in the skies."   *Selah* (Ps. 89:35–37)

The psalmist then goes on to comment on God's apparent repudiation of his promise.

> But now you have cast off and rejected;
>   you are full of wrath against your anointed.
> You have renounced the covenant with your servant;
>   you have defiled his crown in the dust. (vv. 38–39)

He describes the way Jerusalem's enemies are crowing over the fall of the Davidic house (vv. 41–42) and the shame that the exiled king faces. But the psalmist cannot believe this is God's last word: he must be going to keep his promise.

> Lord, where is your steadfast love of old,
>   which by your faithfulness you swore to David? (v. 49)

The answer to this question is given in the next two books

of the Psalms. Book 4 looks back at the Mosaic era by recounting the history of Israel's disobedience and God's forgiveness of
them in that era. This gives the reader of the Psalms hope that the
same could happen again (Psalms 95, 103, 105–6). The last verse
of book 4 before its doxology says,

> Save us, O LORD our God,
>> and gather us from among the nations,
> that we may give thanks to your holy name
>> and glory in your praise. (Ps. 106:47)

This hope is fostered by another recurrent theme in book 4, the
reign of God. Psalm 93 begins, "The LORD reigns." Psalm 95:3 cries,

> For the LORD is a great God,
>> and a great King above all gods.

His reign is universal: he reigns over nature, over Israel, indeed over
all peoples.

> Say among the nations, "The LORD reigns!
>> Yes, the world is established; it shall never be moved;
>> he will judge the peoples with equity." (Ps. 96:10)

In the previous chapter I mentioned that some canonical readers, including such experts as Wilson and McCann, think that
the reign of God is the answer to the end of the Davidic dynasty:
God's ultimate victory makes the restoration of the throne of
David superfluous.

Now I do not want to belittle the reality of this hope in God's
future victorious reign, but given the very vivid way the promises
to David are set out in Psalms 2, 72, and 89 at such prominent
places in the Psalter, I think it is more likely that the psalmist
believed God's reign would be demonstrated by his keeping his
promises to David about an eternal dynasty and all nations serving
him. But had the Psalter ended with book 4 (Psalm 106), I would

regard this arguable but not proved. It is the return of two collections of Davidic psalms in book 5 (108–10, 138–45) and in particular Psalms 110 and 132 that demonstrate that these points are
still valid.

Psalm 110 is often compared with Psalm 2. Both seem to be
coronation psalms promising the new king universal sovereignty.

> The LORD sends forth from Zion
>> your mighty scepter.
>> Rule in the midst of your enemies! (Ps. 110:2; cf. 2:8–9)

Psalm 110 uniquely speaks of the king being a priest like Melchizedek. This allusion to the episode in Genesis 14 is intriguing. But
for our argument the mode in which the promise is couched is
striking.

> The LORD has sworn
>> and will not change his mind,
> "You are a priest forever
>> after the order of Melchizedek." (Ps. 110:4)

God's oath is unchangeable. But the divine oath par excellence
is the oath to David. Psalm 89 mentions it 3 times.

> You have said, "I have made a covenant with my chosen one;
>> I have sworn to David my servant:
> 'I will establish your offspring forever,
>> and build your throne for all generations.'" (vv. 3–4)

> Once for all I have sworn by my holiness;
>> I will not lie to David. (v. 35)

> Lord, where is your steadfast love of old,
>> which by your faithfulness you swore to David? (v. 49)

If God has promised to keep his otherwise unknown oath
about the priesthood of Melchizedek, it must surely be expected

that he will keep his much better known oath that David's sons will always occupy his throne. Psalm 132:11–12 makes this point explicitly.

> The LORD swore to David a sure oath
>> from which he will not turn back:
> "One of the sons of your body
>> I will set on your throne.
> If your sons keep my covenant
>> and my testimonies that I shall teach them,
> their sons also forever
>> shall sit on your throne."

The conditional clause "if your sons keep my covenant" explains the interruption of the dynasty, but it does not rule out hope for its restoration, as the last verses make plain. The choice of Zion as God's dwelling place is forever (v. 14).

> There I will make a horn to sprout for David;
>> I have prepared a lamp for my anointed. (v. 17)

Finally, Psalm 145, the last of the psalms ascribed to David, sounds very optimistic. It would hardly fit if he expected the extinction of his dynasty.

> I will extol you, my God and King,
>> and bless your name forever and ever. . . .
>
> Your kingdom is an everlasting kingdom,
>> and your dominion endures throughout all generations.
>
> The LORD is faithful in all his words
>> and kind in all his works. (Ps. 145:1, 13)

For these reasons it seems to me probable that the editors of the Psalter did hope for a revival of the Davidic house. They were not expecting just a spiritual reign of God without tangible results.

In other words, they read the royal psalms as prophecies, not just as prayers for the old Davidic house that God had failed to answer.

But as we know, the New Testament does not just read the royal psalms prophetically; it also understands many of the laments prophetically, most obviously Psalm 22. Is this a purely New Testament understanding, or does the arrangement of the Psalter also hint in this direction? In the previous chapter I mentioned the way Miller and Kleer have related the psalms attributed to David to the messianic theme of the Pentateuch, and I should like to develop this point a little now.

Davidic Psalms: A Closer Look

Of the seventy-three psalms entitled "A Psalm of David," or something similar, thirteen[23] have titles that explain the circumstances of the psalms' composition: for example, Psalm 34: "Of David, when he changed his behavior before Abimelech, so that he drove him out, and he went away." Kleer points out that these historical tidbits nearly all refer to the problem eras in David's life: his persecution by Saul (Psalms 18, 34, 52, 54, 56–57, 59, 63, 142), Absalom's rebellion (Psalm 3), his sin with Bathsheba (Psalm 51), and his problems with Cush (Psalm 7). Most of these episodes are referred to in the books of Samuel, not the parallel accounts in the books of Chronicles. A similar picture of someone in trouble is painted by many of the other psalms of David: they are mostly a mixture of laments during distress, and thanksgivings after being rescued from a problem. In the first book of the Psalter the following may be classed as laments:[24] Psalms 3–7, 10–14, 16–17, 20, 22, 25–28, 31, 35–36, 38–39. Thanksgivings include 9, 18, 30, 32, 34, 40–41.

These psalms record the appeals for help by a righteous man persecuted by his enemies. For example:

> The LORD judges the peoples;
>> judge me, O LORD, according to my righteousness

---

[23] Psalms 3, 7, 18, 34, 51, 52, 54, 56, 57, 59, 60, 63, 142.
[24] Classification is not always clear: see Johnston and Firth, *Interpreting the Psalms*, 296–300.

and according to the integrity that is in me.
Oh, let the evil of the wicked come to an end,
and may you establish the righteous—
you who test the minds and hearts,
O righteous God! (Ps. 7:8–9)

David continues to assert his righteousness and his expectation that God will intervene on his behalf.

My shield is with God,
who saves the upright in heart. (v. 10)

Now as Miller has pointed out, this philosophy that God will vindicate the righteous and punish the wicked is very much the theme of Psalm 1.

Therefore the wicked will not stand in the judgment,
nor sinners in the congregation of the righteous;
for the Lord knows the way of the righteous,
but the way of the wicked will perish. (Ps. 1:5–6)

The titles of these psalms ascribe them to David, so in reading them we are supposed to identify the plaintiff with him. He is the aggrieved party pleading before the righteous Judge for justice.

God is a righteous judge,
and a God who feels indignation every day. (Ps. 7:11)

Usually these laments end with a testimony by David that God has listened to his complaint. For example:

The Lord has heard my plea;
the Lord accepts my prayer.
All my enemies shall be ashamed and greatly troubled;
they shall turn back and be put to shame in a moment.
(Ps. 6:9–10)

Thus the book of the Psalms presents us with two pictures of the Davidic house: the first is expressed in Psalms 2, 72, 110, and 132. They show the ideal: the son of David who is also the Son of God, to whom all the nations bow down (72:11; 110:1). The second is found in the Davidic laments and thanksgivings, which—as we have just seen—picture a suffering David, who survives unjust assaults from his enemies only by the gracious intervention of God. We have suggested that the first picture of the all-conquering king outshines any historical reality, and that the highlighting of this figure in a time when Israel had no king must indicate that the editors at least understood these psalms prophetically. Does this also apply to the other set of pictures of the innocent sufferer David?

We have noted that the historical fragments included in some of the psalm titles relate to episodes in the books of Samuel. These surely invite us to contrast David's character portrayed in these psalms with the David described in the books of Samuel. And from time to time one feels that the pious claims of the psalmic David perhaps do not quite gel with the David we meet in the books of Samuel. For example,

> O LORD my God, if I have done this,
>   if there is wrong in my hands,
> if I have repaid my friend with evil
>   or plundered my enemy without cause,
> let the enemy pursue my soul and overtake it,
>   and let him trample my life to the ground
>   and lay my glory in the dust. (Ps. 7:3–5)

In a number of incidents in the books of Samuel, David did not act quite as honorably as this. Overall the books show how he squandered his promising start. His misbehavior led to Absalom's rebellion, on the one hand, and the later attempted coup by Adonijah, on the other hand. A number of episodes earlier in the story may well give us hints of David's incipient moral decline.

Clearly, the editors of the Psalms knew the account in 1 and 2 Samuel, and they were probably conscious that the historical

David did not always behave like the implied David of the Psalms. So I wonder whether this led them to read the Davidic laments and thanksgivings as prophetic too. They evidently did so with the royal psalms such as 2 and 72. Might they not have been thinking similarly about such psalms as 3–7, 9–13, 22, and so on?

I leave that as a question. But if we do put the two pictures together—the ideal king with universal sovereignty, and the innocent suffering David—we arrive at the picture of a David who through suffering inherits a universal kingdom. It is the vision of his mission that Jesus expounded to the two disciples on the way to Emmaus: "'Was it not necessary that the Christ should suffer these things and enter into his glory?' And beginning with Moses and all the Prophets, he interpreted to them in all the Scriptures the things concerning himself" (Luke 24:26–27).

There has been much discussion as to how Jesus came to understand that his role would be that of a suffering Messiah, when the common first-century Jewish expectation was that the Messiah would be a conquering king. Scholars usually look to Isaiah 53 to explain the scriptural basis of his conviction. But recent study of the Psalms, as I have shown, perhaps points to another source. The juxtaposition of the triumphant king in Psalm 2 with the persecuted David in Psalms 3 onward could also lead to the conclusion that the future David would suffer before he triumphed.

This I believe was the understanding of the editors of the psalms. Their careful arrangement of the psalms gives us sufficient clues for reconstructing their understanding. But this represents an interpretation of the psalms as they were read perhaps in the fifth century BC. Was this the way the original authors, David or otherwise, understood them when they composed them several centuries earlier? We cannot know.

I am inclined to think that originally many of these psalms were not understood messianically. I do jib at Augustine's reading of "I lay down and slept; I woke again, for the LORD sustained me" as a prophecy of the resurrection. A straightforward historical interpretation of the psalmist's testimony to God's continuing protection seems quite adequate to me in this case. But that is not to say that a historical interpretation is the last word. It is common in the New Testament for clearly nonprophetic comments to be understood prophetically. A clear case is Matthew's rereading of Hosea's words,

> When Israel was a child, I loved him,
> and out of Egypt I called my son. (Hos. 11:1)

Matthew says:

> And [Joseph] rose and took the child and his mother by night and departed to Egypt and remained there until the death of Herod. This was to fulfill what the Lord had spoken by the prophet, "Out of Egypt I called my son." (Matt. 2:14–15)

In the prophecy of Hosea this is just a historical comment on the exodus of the Israelites from Egypt. But Matthew, seeing Jesus as the true Israel, applies Hosea's historical comment to the life of Jesus. This is sometimes called *sensus plenior* or fuller sense. The idea is that Scripture has two authors, the human prophet or writer and God who inspired the writer. The writer in this case, Hosea, just thought he was referring to a past event, but God who knew the future was predicting that Jesus would experience an exodus from Egypt too. This fuller sense was apparent to human readers only after the flight into Egypt by the holy family. In this way we can read Hosea's comment on the old exodus as a prophecy about Jesus's experience in Egypt.

This interpretative strategy would explain Psalm 22 quite easily. We can read it historically as a lament of a royal figure on the verge of death with his enemies looking on, hoping for his imminent demise. But the New Testament clearly sees it as more fully realized in the crucifixion. Not only does Jesus cry out, "My God, my God, why have you forsaken me?" but many features of the crucifixion are anticipated in the psalm: the scorn of the bystanders, the casting lots for his clothing, the piercing of his hands and feet. So it is no wonder that the evangelists draw attention to the fulfillment of this psalm. This seems to me an excellent case of *sensus plenior*, of realizing the full meaning of the psalm long after it was first written and the crucifixion had been seen.

Still, if we are right to hold that the editors of the psalms were already thinking of a future suffering David, this would be no ordinary *sensus plenior*, for the editors had not seen the crucifixion. This is akin to true prophecy. The original author of the psalm may have been describing his own experience, but the editors believed he was describing one yet to be revealed.

CHAPTER 5

The Ethics of the Psalms[1]

A hymnbook used at our church includes these lines:

> This is our God, the servant king
>> he calls us now to follow him.
>>> Graham Kendrick

> O thou who camest from above
>> the fire celestial to impart,
> kindle a flame of sacred love
>> on the mean altar of my heart.
>>> Charles Wesley

> He who would true valour see,
>> let him come hither.
>>> John Bunyan

Or even more militantly:

> Stand up stand up for Jesus,
>> ye soldiers of the cross!
> Lift high his royal banner,
>> it must not suffer loss.
> From victory unto victory
>> his army he shall lead
> till every foe is vanquished
>> and Christ is Lord indeed.
>>> George Duffield

---

[1] Originally read at the Tyndale Fellowship Old Testament Group, Cambridge, July 16, 2004; first published in *Interpreting the Psalms: Issues and Approaches*, ed. Philip S. Johnston and David G. Firth, 175–94. Copyright © Inter-Varsity Press 2005. Used by permission of InterVarsity Press, PO Box 1400, Downers Grove, IL 60515. www.ivpress.com.

These hymns are prayers, set to music, that God will work within us to make us what the hymn writers think we ought to be like. Graham Kendrick and Charles Wesley want us to offer ourselves to God completely, as though we were a sacrifice. John Bunyan and George Duffield encourage us to fight for God against the world, the flesh, and the Devil. Through their poetry these writers tell us how to act or, more subtly, make us pray to act. Their words implicitly teach us what to believe and how to behave. And when we sing them, we declare our commitment to these views, and we encourage our fellow worshippers to do the same.

This is sometimes recognized by those who compile hymnals. The newish hymnbook *Hymns Old and New* explains in its introduction that some ancient hymns are unsuitable for modern worship because they put over some ideas incompatible with modern thought. It was not just nonfeminist ideas that the compilers disliked, but the militarism of some hymns.[2] Consequently, "Stand Up, Stand Up for Jesus" was completely rewritten, while "Onward Christian Soldiers" has become "Onward Christian Pilgrims"! But "Dear Lord and Father of Mankind" did survive, despite its quasi-Buddhist lines:

Breathe through the heats of our desire
thy coolness and thy balm.
Let sense be dumb, let flesh retire . . .

And, of course, the prayer of St. Francis "Make Me a Channel of Your Peace" was included.

Now, though I do not endorse the compilers' principles of

---

[2] "We were also concerned that the book should use positive and appropriate images, and decided that militarism and triumphalism were, therefore, not appropriate. We recognise that military imagery is used in the Bible, but history, including current events, shows only too clearly the misuse to which those images are open. All too often in the Christian and other religions, texts advocating spiritual warfare are used to justify the self-serving ambitions behind temporal conflicts. Christian 'triumph' is the triumph of love which 'is not envious or boastful or arrogant' (1 Corinthians 13:4): the triumph of the cross" (Foreword to *Hymns Old and New: New Anglican Edition* [Bury St Edmunds: Kevin Mayhew, 1996]). Another fundamental principle was the use of inclusive language in referring to the human race. Only rare exceptions were made after much deliberation (ibid., 3).

selection, I do think they are right to notice the teaching function of hymns and indeed liturgy in general. I remember my tutor on early Christian doctrine stressing *lex orandi, lex credendi*—the worshipper's central beliefs are expressed in his prayers. A study of the Lord's Prayer may be just as informative about Christian theology as, say, the much longer Apostles' Creed, for it is in prayer that people give utterance to their deepest and most fundamental convictions. Thus the words hymn writers and liturgists put on our lips in worship affect us profoundly: they teach us what to think and feel, the more effectively as they are put to music so we can hum them to ourselves whenever we are inclined.

Particularly influential in this regard are the Psalms, which have been at the heart of Jewish and Christian worship for the best part of three millennia.[3] Sung first in the temple, then in the apostolic churches, the Psalms constituted the core diet of the monastic tradition, on the one hand, and the Reformed tradition, on the other. It is only a relatively recent phenomenon that hymns have displaced psalms as the mainspring of Christian worship. If the *lex orandi, lex credendi* principle is correct, the Psalms must have had the most profound effect on Christian theology and ethics.

But though the theology of the Psalms has often been discussed,[4] I have noted very little work devoted to their ethics. For instance, three recent works on Old Testament ethics more or less overlook the contribution of the Psalms. Eckart Otto's *Theologische Ethik des Alten Testaments* (1994) has just thirteen references to the Psalms, compared with forty to Proverbs and seventy-eight to Deuteronomy, although the book of the Psalms is about three times as long as Proverbs or Deuteronomy. A similar disproportion is noticeable in Cyril S. Rodd's *Glimpses of a Strange Land: Studies in Old Testament Ethics* (2001), which has double the number of references to Deuteronomy and to Proverbs as it has to the Psalms. A slight improvement is visible in Christopher

---

[3] See William L. Holladay, *The Psalms through Three Thousand Years* (Minneapolis: Fortress, 1993).
[4] E.g., Hans-Joachim Kraus, *Theology of the Psalms*, trans. Keith Crim (Minneapolis: Fortress, 1992).

Wright's *Old Testament Ethics for the People of God* (2004), but still there are 50 percent more references to Deuteronomy than to the Psalms.

This scholarly blind spot is the more surprising in that the Psalter begins with Psalm 1, which invites the reader to meditate on the law day and night. Careful examination of the psalm suggests that the law the psalmist had in mind is not just the law of Moses, but the Psalter itself, which probably has been deliberately divided into five books to mimic the Pentateuch.[5] That the law is so important is underlined by the presence of Psalm 119, the longest psalm, with its repeated refrain "Teach me your statutes" (vv. 12, 26, 64, 68, 124, 135, 171) and similar prayers (vv. 29, "law"; 33, "way of your statutes"; 66, "good judgment and knowledge"; 108, "rules"). While some commentators have noted these phenomena, there has been a tendency to downplay them, ascribing them to a later wisdom redactor who, because he is alleged to be late, is *ipso facto* unimportant. In this chapter I want to start to remedy this neglect by drawing out the pervasiveness of ethical concern in the Psalter and making a preliminary evaluation of its potential for Old Testament ethics.

But I should like to stress that this seems to be virgin scholarly territory. Not only is the topic rarely touched on in works on Old Testament ethics, but I have been able to find very few articles that discuss our topic. Discussion rarely gets beyond the entrance liturgies of Psalms 15 and 24, the imprecatory psalms, or the ideals of kingship in Psalm 72.[6] So how should we proceed?

---

[5] The Hebrew Old Testament is divided into three sections: Law (Genesis–Deuteronomy), Prophets (Joshua–Malachi), and Writings (Psalms–Chronicles). It is striking that right at the beginning of both the Prophets and the Writings there is explicit encouragement to meditate on the Law. Joshua is told: "This Book of the Law shall not depart from your mouth, but you shall meditate on it day and night, so that you may be careful to do according to all that is written in it. For then you will make your way prosperous, and then you will have good success" (Josh. 1:8). Ps. 1:2–3 seems clearly to allude to this verse.

[6] E.g., Walter J. Houston, "The King's Preferential Option for the Poor: Rhetoric, Ideology and Ethics in Psalm 72," *Biblical Interpretation* 7 (1999): 341–67; Ronald E. Clements, "Worship and Ethics: A Re-examination of Psalm 15," in *Worship in the Hebrew Bible: Essays in Honor of John T. Willis*, ed. M. P. Graham, R. R. Marrs, and S. L. McKenzie (Sheffield: Sheffield Academic Press, 1999), 78–94; and Erich Zenger, *A God of Vengeance? Understanding the Psalms of Divine Wrath*, trans. Linda M. Maloney (Louisville: Westminster John Knox, 1996).

If the Ten Commandments are the quintessence of biblical ethics, it might be appropriate to start by seeing when and where they are alluded to or quoted. Are there any direct quotes? Which topics in the Decalogue—idolatry, theft, etc.—are most often mentioned in the Psalms, and which are omitted? From an examination of the rules endorsed by the Psalms, we shall turn to the lifestyle they commend. What should the righteous be like? How may their character be defined in terms of virtues, and what are the typical vices of the wicked?

(The Psalms are first and foremost prayers, so they constantly bring God into the picture, not least in their ethical statements. God's character is constantly appealed to as the guarantor of the ethical system: he will ensure that the wicked are punished and the righteous are rewarded.)But more than that, God's actions are often seen as a model for human behavior. His care for the downtrodden and oppressed and his hatred of duplicity should inspire all his human subjects in their attitudes toward others. Finally, I wish to say a little about *hesed*, steadfast love, one of the favorite terms in the Psalms to describe God's character.

The Psalms and the Decalogue

Though the law in general (see Psalms 1, 19, 119) and individual laws in particular are so important in the Psalter, it is surprising how rarely the law giving at Sinai is mentioned. In fact, in the long psalms reciting Israel's history it is usually omitted. The plagues of Egypt are mentioned, as are the exodus, wilderness wanderings, and conquest of Canaan, but the law giving is notable by its absence (Psalms 78, 105–7, 114). In fact Sinai is explicitly named only in Psalm 68 (vv. 8, 17), and Horeb in Psalm 106:19. However, though the law giving may not be mentioned at the most appropriate place in the historical sequence, it clearly is presupposed. Psalm 78 essentially demonstrates how Israel has persistently neglected the law they were given and told to teach to their children.

> He established a testimony in Jacob
>> and appointed a law in Israel,
> which he commanded our fathers
>> to teach to their children,
> that the next generation might know them,
>> the children yet unborn,
> and arise and tell them to their children,
>> so that they should set their hope in God
> and not forget the works of God,
>> but keep his commandments;
> and that they should not be like their fathers,
>> a stubborn and rebellious generation,
> a generation whose heart was not steadfast,
>> whose spirit was not faithful to God. (vv. 5–8)

Similarly, though Psalm 105 says nothing about the law giving in its historical review, it ends,

> And he gave them the lands of the nations,
>> and they took possession of the fruit of the peoples' toil,
> that they might keep his statutes
>> and observe his laws.
> Praise the Lord! (vv. 44–45)

These reviews of Israel's past are thus designed to produce a sense of gratitude and therefore willingness to observe the law (so Psalm 105), or to highlight Israel's treachery in failing to keep it (Psalm 78).

The much shorter history in Psalm 81 is different. It not only quotes the prologue to the Ten Commandments,

> I am the LORD your God,
>> who brought you up[7] out of the land of Egypt. (Ps. 81:10)

It also paraphrases the first two commandments:

---

[7] Exodus has "brought out" (*hotsi'*), whereas Psalm 81 has "brought up" (*ha'alah*).

> There shall be no strange god among you;
>> you shall not bow down to a foreign god. (Ps. 81:9)

Compare Exodus 20:3–5: "You shall have no other gods before me. You shall not make for yourself a carved image, or any likeness of anything that is in heaven above, or that is in the earth beneath, or that is in the water under the earth. You shall not bow down to them or serve them."

I have not noted any other close quotation of the first commandment, but the stress on God's uniqueness and/or supremacy over other gods is frequent. For example:

> There is none like you among the gods, O Lord,
>> nor are there any works like yours. . . .
> For you are great and do wondrous things;
>> you alone are God. (Ps. 86:8, 10; cf. 95:3; 96:4; 97:9)

Also affirming the first commandment are the declarations of complete dependence on the one God.

The second commandment, banning idolatry, is reaffirmed strongly too.

> Who shall ascend the hill of the LORD?
>> And who shall stand in his holy place?
> He who has clean hands and a pure heart,
>> who does not lift up his soul to what is false
>> and does not swear deceitfully. (Ps. 24:3–4)

"What is false" (*shav'*) is usually supposed to be a reference to idolatry,[8] though the phraseology is closer to the third commandment: "You shall not take the name of the LORD your God in vain, for the LORD will not hold him guiltless who takes his name in vain." (Ex. 20:7)

---

[8] E.g., A. F. Kirkpatrick, *The Book of Psalms* (Cambridge: Cambridge University Press, 1902); and Hans-Joachim Kraus, *Psalmen 1–59* (Neukirchen: Neukirchener Verlag, 2003); but Klaus Seybold, *Die Psalmen* (Tübingen: Mohr, 1996), prefers to connect it to Ex. 20:7.

However, there is no mistaking the robust assault on idolatry in Psalms 115//135.

> Why should the nations say,
>   "Where is their God?"
> Our God is in the heavens;
>   he does all that he pleases.
>
> Their idols are silver and gold,
>   the work of human hands.
> They have mouths, but do not speak;
>   eyes, but do not see.
> They have ears, but do not hear;
>   noses, but do not smell.
> They have hands, but do not feel;
>   feet, but do not walk;
>   and they do not make a sound in their throat.
> Those who make them become like them;
>   so do all who trust in them. (Ps. 115:2–8; cf. 135:15–18)

Psalm 31:6 sums up the attitude of the Psalter.

> I hate those who pay regard to worthless idols,
>   but I trust in the Lord. (cf. 44:20; 81:9; 97:7; 106:36)

The third commandment, "You shall not take the name of the LORD your God in vain" (Ex. 20:7), is not directly quoted in the Psalms, unless 24:4 is an allusion to it, but the proper use of God's name is frequently celebrated.[9] Psalm 8 is devoted to this topic.

> O LORD, our Lord,
>   how majestic is your name in all the earth! (Ps. 8:1, 9)

Other typical sentiments in the Psalms are

---

[9] *THWAT* 2:937 gives 106 uses in the Psalms out of 778 in the whole Old Testament.

> Ascribe to the LORD the glory due his name;
>> bring an offering, and come into his courts! (Ps. 96:8)

> Let them praise your great and awesome name!
>> Holy is he! (Ps. 99:3)

The Psalms underline the importance of the name by illustrating how it ought to be used, not by expressly banning its misuse. If God's name were honored in the way the Psalms do, there would be no question of taking it in vain.

The only commandment that seems to be ignored by the Psalms is Exodus 20:8, "Remember the Sabbath day, to keep it holy." There is one psalm (92) whose heading is "A Song for the Sabbath,"[10] and Psalm 81:3 urges,

> Blow the trumpet at the new moon,
>> at the full moon, on our feast day.

But nowhere else is there a mention of the obligation to remember the Sabbath. Psalm 95:7, "Today, if you hear his voice," and Psalm 118:24, "This is the day that the LORD has made," clearly refer to the day on which these psalms are being sung, which could be the Sabbath. Given the importance of the Sabbath in the pre-exilic era, when most of the psalms were composed, and in the postexilic era, when they were collected (Amos 8:5; Isa. 1:13; Neh. 13:15–22), the celebration of the Sabbath must be presupposed by the Psalter. But why it is not explicitly mentioned is not obvious. It could be that it is assumed that the Psalms were for use on the Sabbath by worshippers in the temple, so they did not need reminding. Alternatively, the Psalms may reflect a popular lay piety that encouraged their use anywhere and at any time.

Exodus 20:12, "Honor your father and your mother, that your days may be long in the land that the LORD your God is giving you," is another commandment that at first sight seems not to matter in

---

[10] Psalms 38 is said in the Septuagint (Psalm 37) to be "for the memorial offering *of the Sabbath*."

the Psalms. However, the gift of children and the privilege of parenthood are very much celebrated in the Psalter, not to mention the land promise. Just as the name of God is celebrated in the Psalms and its profanation barely mentioned, so the Psalms celebrate the family dimension of life. God is the archetypal Father: this in itself implies that earthly fathers should be honored. For example,

> He shall cry to me, "You are my Father,
> my God, and the Rock of my salvation." (Ps. 89:26)

God's blessing is shown in the gift of children: a big family is to be treasured.

> Behold, children are a heritage from the LORD,
> the fruit of the womb a reward. (Ps. 127:3)

If the fourth and fifth commandments are relatively underplayed in the Psalter, the prohibition of murder is quite frequently alluded to, even if some remarks do not imply literal killing so much as depriving someone of his livelihood. Enemies are compared to savage lions or dogs rending their prey (Pss. 7:2; 17:12; 22:13, 16; 35:17), or to bulls (22:12), or to a highwayman (10:8), who watches for the righteous and seeks to put him to death (37:32; cf. 54:3; 70:2). The wicked also kill the widow and the sojourner, and murder the fatherless (94:6). These accusations are mostly embedded in laments, pleas to God to prevent or avenge such crimes.

Adultery is mentioned explicitly only once in the Psalms.[11]

> But to the wicked God says:
> "What right have you to recite my statutes
> or take my covenant on your lips?
> For you hate discipline,
> and you cast my words behind you.

---

[11] Whereas the prophets frequently speak of Israel "whoring" (zanah) after other gods, the Psalms use this image only twice (Pss. 73:27; 106:39).

If you see a thief, you are pleased with him,
    and you keep company with adulterers.

"You give your mouth free rein for evil,
    and your tongue frames deceit." (Ps. 50:16–19)

The condemnation of adultery is here linked to a rejection of God's statutes, covenant, and "words" (the Hebrew term for the Decalogue means "ten words," Ex. 34:28), and a string of offenses—theft, adultery, and false witness—that make it clear that the psalmist is consciously recalling the Ten Commandments.

Although Psalm 50 has the only explicit reference to adultery in the Psalter, it stands next to Psalm 51, the most moving of all the penitential psalms, which is entitled, "To the choirmaster. A Psalm of David, when Nathan the prophet went to him, after he had gone in to Bathsheba." It begins,

Have mercy on me, O God,
    according to your steadfast love;
according to your abundant mercy
    blot out my transgressions. (51:1)

Now, whatever may be the origin of the psalm and its heading, readings that take seriously the canonical sequence of the psalms and their headings cannot fail to observe what a powerful statement Psalm 51 is about the sin of adultery.

Theft and coveting are also frequently bemoaned in the Psalms. We have already noted the string of theft, adultery, and lying in Psalm 50:18. But stealing, especially from the poor, is condemned often elsewhere.

For the wicked boasts of the desires of his soul,
    and the one greedy for gain curses and renounces the
        LORD. . . .
he lurks in ambush like a lion in his thicket;
he lurks that he may seize the poor;

he seizes the poor when he draws him into his net.
(Ps. 10:3, 9)

"Because the poor are plundered, because the needy groan,
I will now arise," says the LORD;
"I will place him in the safety for which he longs." (Ps. 12:5;
see also 14:4; 22:18; 26:4, 10; 69:4)

But of all the sins in the Decalogue, it is surely the ninth commandment that receives the fullest treatment: "You shall not bear
false witness against your neighbor" (Ex. 20:16). Verse after verse
condemns the misuse of the tongue.

O men, how long shall my honor be turned into shame?
How long will you love vain words and seek after lies?
(Ps. 4:2)

You destroy those who speak lies;
the LORD abhors the bloodthirsty and deceitful man. . . .

For there is no truth in their mouth;
their inmost self is destruction;
their throat is an open grave;
they flatter with their tongue. (Ps. 5:6, 9)

His mouth is filled with cursing and deceit and oppression;
under his tongue are mischief and iniquity. (Ps. 10:7)

Everyone utters lies to his neighbor;
with flattering lips and a double heart they speak. (Ps. 12:2)

He who walks blamelessly and does what is right
and speaks truth in his heart;
who does not slander with his tongue
and does no evil to his neighbor,
nor takes up a reproach against his friend;
in whose eyes a vile person is despised,

but who honors those who fear the LORD;
who swears to his own hurt and does not change.
(Ps. 15:2–4)

(Further examples are Pss. 27:12; 28:3; 34:13; 35:11, 20; 50:19–20; 52:2–5; 56:9–11, 21; 59:12; 64:3–5; 66:13–14; 69:4; 73:8–9; 101:5; 109:2; 120:2–3; 140:3; 144:11.)

The abundance of passages on this topic is a surprise. Why should this topic be so important, whereas the Sabbath is so neglected? It is not clear, but three observations may put this feature in perspective. First, the book of Proverbs also frequently highlights the use and abuse of speech. Second, the Psalms are most concerned about interpersonal behavior—about honesty, integrity, and good neighborliness, all of which may be destroyed by ill-considered words. Third, the Psalms themselves are examples of the positive use of the tongue for the praise of God. This makes the tongue's negative use to destroy one's fellow man especially reprehensible. As James puts it: "With it we bless our Lord and Father, and with it we curse people who are made in the likeness of God. From the same mouth come blessing and cursing. My brothers, these things ought not to be so" (James 3:9–10).

The Righteous and the Wicked

So far I have just tried to show how the Psalter supports the principles of the Decalogue. This is only one string to its ethical bow. Indeed, I think it is secondary to its chief approach to presenting ethics, which is through the description of the good and the wicked, or, in Hebrew terminology, the righteous and the wicked. (Hebrew *tov*, traditionally translated "good," is rarely used of human character.) The two ways of the righteous and the wicked are presented in the very first psalm.

Blessed is the man
who walks not in the counsel of the wicked,
nor stands in the way of sinners,
nor sits in the seat of scoffers;

but his delight is in the law of the LORD,
    and on his law he meditates day and night.

He is like a tree
    planted by streams of water
that yields its fruit in its season,
    and its leaf does not wither.
In all that he does, he prospers.
The wicked are not so,
    but are like chaff that the wind drives away.

Therefore the wicked will not stand in the judgment,
    nor sinners in the congregation of the righteous;
for the LORD knows the way of the righteous,
    but the way of the wicked will perish.

There are two types of people, two types of life, and two conclusions. Which will you choose to follow? is the question posed by
Psalm 1. Its own answer is clear, but the following psalms develop
this contrast between the wicked and the righteous very fully. Time
and again the Psalms declare that the righteous enjoy God's favor
(5:12; 7:9; 14:5; 34:15; 37:17, 29; 112:6). God answers their prayers
(34:15, 17) and delivers them from the plots of the wicked (37:39).

But what characterizes the righteous, besides meditating on
the law and dissociating himself from the wicked (Ps. 1:1–3)?
Psalm 112 amplifies the picture.

Praise the LORD!
Blessed is the man who fears the LORD,
    who greatly delights in his commandments! . . .
Light dawns in the darkness for the upright;
    he is gracious, merciful, and righteous.
It is well with the man who deals generously and lends;
    who conducts his affairs with justice.
For the righteous will never be moved;
    he will be remembered forever.
He is not afraid of bad news;

his heart is firm, trusting in the LORD.
His heart is steady; he will not be afraid,
  until he looks in triumph on his adversaries.
He has distributed freely; he has given to the poor;
  his righteousness endures forever;
  his horn is exalted in honor. (Ps. 112:1, 4–9)

Though study of the law is one aspect of the righteous person's character, this passage also highlights his trust in God (vv. 1, 7–8), as well as his generosity (vv. 5, 9).

It is important to note that though the righteous enjoy ultimate prosperity and vindication, they may well have to suffer in the short term. The many laments in the Psalter are prayers of the righteous who are suffering from illness, oppression, and persecution (e.g., Psalms 3–7).

The wicked, on the other hand, are the converse of the righteous. The Psalms emphasize that they will ultimately perish (Pss. 1:6; 3:7; 9:5, 16–17; 34:21; 68:2; 101:8; 146:9; 147:6). In the short term the wicked may appear to flourish, but that is misleading.

For I was envious of the arrogant
  when I saw the prosperity of the wicked.

For they have no pangs until death;
  their bodies are fat and sleek.
They are not in trouble as others are;
  they are not stricken like the rest of mankind.
Therefore pride is their necklace;
  violence covers them as a garment.
Their eyes swell out through fatness;
  their hearts overflow with follies.
They scoff and speak with malice;
  loftily they threaten oppression.
They set their mouths against the heavens,
  and their tongue struts through the earth.
Therefore his people turn back to them,
  and find no fault in them.

And they say, "How can God know?
>   Is there knowledge in the Most High?"
Behold, these are the wicked;
>   always at ease, they increase in riches. . . .
Truly you set them in slippery places;
>   you make them fall to ruin.
How they are destroyed in a moment,
>   swept away utterly by terrors! (Ps. 73:3–12, 18–19)

The wicked are the converse of the righteous. Whereas the righteous fear God, the wicked mock him. Whereas the righteous are generous to the poor, the wicked exploit the poor, impoverishing them further.

The wicked draw the sword and bend their bows
>   to bring down the poor and needy,
>   to slay those whose way is upright; . . .

The wicked borrows but does not pay back,
>   but the righteous is generous and gives; . . .

The wicked watches for the righteous
>   and seeks to put him to death. . . .

I have seen a wicked, ruthless man,
>   spreading himself like a green laurel tree.
But he passed away, and behold he was no more;
>   though I sought him, he could not be found.
>   (Ps. 37:14, 21, 32, 35–36)

The wicked pays lip service to God's law but does not practice it (50:16). He is boastful and scheming, and bears grudges (55:3; 64:2; 75:4).

God as Guarantor of Judgment

The Psalms are direct addresses to God. They are prayers of faith expressing the psalmists' conviction that God reigns, that he is the ultimate Judge. Even the laments, which start in despair, end in hope. The kingship psalms, 93–100, which celebrate the fact that the Lord reigns, often end with the affirmation that God will judge the earth and that this is cause for celebration.

> Let the heavens be glad, and let the earth rejoice;
>> let the sea roar, and all that fills it;
>> let the field exult, and everything in it!
> Then shall all the trees of the forest sing for joy
>> before the LORD, for he comes,
>> for he comes to judge the earth.
> He will judge the world in righteousness,
>> and the peoples in his faithfulness. (Ps. 96:11–13)

This is rarely our reaction to the thought of God's coming in judgment, but it recurs frequently throughout the Psalter. As Zenger has pointed out, that God will be the universal Judge is a message of hope in a world of oppression and injustice.[12] The Psalms look forward to a universal judgment, but also to particular, more immediate judgment on the wicked and their activities.

Psalm 1:6 declares that the way of the wicked will perish. In Psalm 2 the kings of the earth plot against the Lord and his anointed, but God will dash them in pieces like a potter's vessel (2:1–9). Psalm 3:7 affirms of God, "You break the teeth of the wicked," while Psalm 5:6 affirms,

> You destroy those who speak lies;
>> the LORD abhors the bloodthirsty and deceitful man.

Psalm 6 ends with this triumphant cry of faith:

> The LORD has heard my plea;
>> the LORD accepts my prayer.
> All my enemies shall be ashamed and greatly troubled;
>> they shall turn back and be put to shame in a moment.
>> (vv. 9–10)

---

[12] Zenger, *God of Vengeance?*, 63–86.

And Psalm 7 pictures the wicked catching himself out.

> He makes a pit, digging it out,
>> and falls into the hole that he has made.
> His mischief returns upon his own head,
>> and on his own skull his violence descends. (vv. 15–16)

This sounds like nasty vindictiveness, *Schadenfreude*, celebrating your enemies' suffering, their comeuppance. But if we look at it through the eyes of the sufferers, we might feel this impression is an over-harsh judgment. Commenting on one of the harshest imprecatory psalms, McCann says:

> Psalm 109 not only tells it like it is with us, but it also tells us how it is with the world. The psalmist had been victimized; and when persons become victims, they are bound to react with rage. . . . When persons are treated unjustly, we can expect them to lash out; we can expect them to express vehemently the desire for an end to the violence that has made them a victim.[13]

But we could see these remarks as making a moral statement regarding the person uttering them, though in a more subtle fashion than some of the hymns I quoted at the beginning. If someone rejoices in the fact that God will dash the wicked in pieces like a potter's vessel, he is implicitly putting himself firmly on God's side and committing himself not to do anything that would put him in the class of the wicked.[14] The moral implications of reciting these remarks about divine judgment are thus immense. To rejoice in God's judgment on sin is to turn the spotlight on one's own life and behavior: will I pass muster with God? Such questions become

---

[13] J. Clinton McCann Jr., *A Theological Introduction to the Book of Psalms* (Nashville: Abingdon Press, 1993), 114.

[14] Anthony C. Thiselton, *New Horizons in Hermeneutics* (London: HarperCollins, 1992), 299, points out that in worship many statements are performative speech acts. To say, "I give thanks to Thee, O LORD, with my whole heart" is not merely informing God about one's feelings, but also performing an act of thanksgiving in itself. This observation, though based on modern speech-act theory, is not new. Athanasius discusses it in his letter to Marcellinus. A helpful modern discussion is Harry Nasuti, "The Sacramental Function of the Psalms in Contemporary Scholarship and Liturgical Practice," in *Psalms and Practice*, ed. Stephen B. Reid (Collegeville, MN: Liturgical Press, 2001), 78–89.

particularly acute when we recite Psalm 14, with its stress on the universality of sin, or sing Psalm 139, with its recognition that we are often unaware that we are sinning. Is this perhaps why traditional Christians who used the Psalms so much lived in such awe of the last judgment?

The Imitation of God as a Principle of the Psalms

In many ways, though not in all, the righteous are supposed to imitate God, who himself is often called righteous (e.g., Pss. 11:7; 116:5). God is the one who is the righteous Judge: he intervenes to save the oppressed, something the righteous should do if they can.

> He raises the poor from the dust
>> and lifts the needy from the ash heap,
> to make them sit with princes,
>> with the princes of his people.
> He gives the barren woman a home,
>> making her the joyous mother of children. (Ps.113:7–9)

Those in the best position to promote righteousness are the kings, and they are called on to exercise godlike qualities of justice.

> Give the king your justice, O God,
>> and your righteousness to the royal son!
> May he judge your people with righteousness,
>> and your poor with justice! . . .
> May he defend the cause of the poor of the people,
>> give deliverance to the children of the needy,
>> and crush the oppressor! (Ps. 72:1–2, 4)

In Psalm 101 king David promises that he will indeed act in a godly way and will see that all his servants meet God's standards. He insists on integrity, loyalty, no backbiting or arrogance, and so on.

> He who walks in the way that is blameless
>> shall minister to me.

No one who practices deceit
    shall dwell in my house;
no one who utters lies
    shall continue before my eyes.

Morning by morning I will destroy
    all the wicked in the land,
cutting off all the evildoers
    from the city of the LORD. (Ps. 101:6–8)

The king is thus expected to identify with God's standards by promoting the righteous and demoting the wicked. But this identification with the divine standpoint extends to everyone who prays the psalms. This emerges in the very first verse of the Psalter.

Blessed is the man
    who walks not in the counsel of the wicked,
nor stands in the way of sinners,
    nor sits in the seat of scoffers. (Ps. 1:1)

But repeatedly the psalmist identifies himself with God's viewpoint: he recites back to God what God thinks. For example:

For you are not a God who delights in wickedness;
    evil may not dwell with you.
The boastful shall not stand before your eyes;
    you hate all evildoers.
You destroy those who speak lies;
    the LORD abhors the bloodthirsty and deceitful man.
        (Ps. 5:4–6)

Running through the Psalms there is an identification of God's standpoint with that of the righteous plaintiff: this is why the psalmist anticipates that God will heed his pleas (cf. Pss. 7:3–5, 9–10; 9:10; 10:12–14; 11:7; 14:5).

Steadfast Love as an Epitome of Psalmic Virtue

This preliminary sketch of psalmic ethics will conclude with a look at a key virtue. Steadfast love (*hesed*) is probably the central aspect of God's character as it is delineated in the Psalms. If the imitation of God is a significant principle in the ethics of the Psalms, it is to be expected that humans should also exhibit *hesed*. We shall investigate this possibility.

Of the 245 occurrences of *hesed* in the Old Testament, 127 are found in the Psalter.[15] Psalm 103:2–4 sums up the essence of *hesed*.

> Bless the LORD, O my soul,
>> and forget not all his benefits,
> who forgives all your iniquity,
>> who heals all your diseases,
> who redeems your life from the pit,
>> who crowns you with steadfast love and mercy.

Hesed is the divine quality behind all God's benevolence: his creation, his forgiveness of sins, his gifts of healing and life. The persistent refrain of Psalm 136, "for his steadfast love endures forever," sums up God's saving activity throughout the Pentateuch as *hesed*. It is demonstrated in the creation (vv. 1–9), in the exodus and wilderness wanderings (vv. 10–16), in the victories in Transjordan and Canaan (vv. 17–22), and in his ongoing support for his people. God's *hesed* is particularly manifest when he answers prayer, a theme of Psalm 107. He brings wanderers home when they cry to him (v. 8), forgives repentant rebels (v. 15), heals those at death's door (v. 21), and rescues drowning sailors (v. 31). All these acts of kindness are triggered by human prayers, but demonstrate God's character of *hesed*.

It is Psalm 103, however, that most reveals what God's *hesed* is like. The psalm alludes to Exodus 34:6–7, which says,

---

[15] *THWAT* 1:601. Useful studies of *hesed* include *THWAT* 1:600–621; *TDOT* 5:44–64; *NIDOTTE* 2:211–18. *Hesed* is often paired with *'emet*, "truth, faithfulness," another key attribute of God's character that man is expected to replicate.

The LORD passed before him and proclaimed, "The LORD, the LORD, a God merciful and gracious, slow to anger, and abounding in steadfast love and faithfulness, keeping steadfast love for thousands, forgiving iniquity and transgression and sin, but who will by no means clear the guilty, visiting the iniquity of the fathers on the children and the children's children, to the third and the fourth generation."

The incident of the golden calf was resolved through God's *hesed*. In response to Moses's prayer appealing to God's promises (Ex. 33:12–16), Israel was spared from annihilation and allowed to proceed to the Promised Land.

So Psalm 103:7–12 brings out the special quality of *hesed*.

He made known his ways to Moses,
     his acts to the people of Israel.
The LORD is merciful and gracious,
     slow to anger and abounding in steadfast love.
He will not always chide,
     nor will he keep his anger forever.
He does not deal with us according to our sins,
     nor repay us according to our iniquities.
For as high as the heavens are above the earth,
     so great is his steadfast love toward those who fear him;
as far as the east is from the west,
     so far does he remove our transgressions from us.

Hesed, "steadfast love," is more than kindness. It has an element of reliability and dependability. It is a permanent feature of God's character. There is a sense of grace about God's willingness to forgive.

Yahweh has decided in favor of Israel; he has promised life, care, alleviation of distress, and preservation—indeed, he has filled the whole earth with his kindness. He has thus granted fellowship with him to his people, to all mankind, to the whole world. And this act, like the promise and assurance of future help and fellowship, is characterized by permanence, constancy, and reliability.[16]

If *hesed* is so important a feature of the divine character, should it not be central to human behavior too? Surprisingly, in the Psalms it is rarely predicated of human beings. An exception is Psalm 109:16.

> For he did not remember to show kindness [*hesed*],
> > but pursued the poor and needy
> > and the brokenhearted, to put them to death.

Because of this man's failure to show *hesed*, the psalmist prays that he will not experience *hesed* himself.

> Let there be none to extend kindness to him,
> > nor any to pity his fatherless children! (Ps. 109:12)

Outside the Psalms numerous passages show that *hesed* is a basic human virtue (e.g., Gen. 20:13; 21:23). The book of Proverbs stresses its importance.

> Let not steadfast love and faithfulness forsake you;
> > bind them around your neck;
> > write them on the tablet of your heart. (Prov. 3:3)

Indeed *hesed* is almost equated with the fear of God in Proverbs 16:6.

> By steadfast love and faithfulness iniquity is atoned for,
> > and by the fear of the LORD one turns away from evil.

So why should it hardly be mentioned as a human virtue in the Psalms? I suggest that it is: the word *hasid* is the adjective derived from *hesed*, and may be translated the one who practices

---

[16] *TDOT* 5:62.

hesed.[17] In fact, this term is even more characteristically concentrated in the Psalms than the noun *hesed*. *Hasid* occurs twenty-five times in the Psalms out of a total thirty-two times in the whole Old Testament. The significance of the term *hasid* may well escape the English reader because it is rendered in a variety of ways in English translations, few of which suggest a relationship with steadfast love or kindness: for example, "merciful," "saint," "godly," "faithful," "kind," "holy." Such a variety of translations for just twenty-five passages means it is easy to overlook.

Only once does the term apply to God in the Psalms.

> The LORD is righteous in all his ways
> and kind [*hasid*] in all his works. (Ps. 145:17)

Another significant passage connecting divine and human expressions of *hasid* is Psalm 18:25.

> With the merciful [*hasid*] you show yourself merciful [verb
> hithpael *hsd*];
> with the blameless man you show yourself blameless.

This passage not only suggests the reciprocal relationship between man and God, but also suggests that man's behavior ought to reflect God's.

But usually the moral dimension is understood rather than expressed. Most often the *hasidim* (faithful saints) are involved in worship (Ps. 30:4), usually singing along with others but sometimes on their beds (Ps. 149:5)! They are in covenant with God (Ps. 50:5). They are contrasted with the wicked (Ps. 37:28). They are those who wait for the Lord and trust in him (Ps. 31:23–24; 86:2).

Conclusion

This chapter has begun an exploration of the ethics inculcated by the Psalms, an area that seems to have been largely overlooked

---

[17] *THWAT* 1:618.

by recent biblical scholarship. It has drawn attention to the self-involving language of worship, the relationship of the Psalms to the Decalogue, and their models of behavior in righteousness and steadfast love. But these are only preliminary observations. They need refining and correcting if this area, which is potentially so important, is to be fully exploited in the study of biblical ethics.

CHAPTER 6

The Imprecatory Psalms[1]

The imprecatory psalms have long been a problem to Bible readers. C. S. Lewis, no advocate of a soft Christianity, wrote:

> In some of the psalms the spirit of hatred which strikes us in the face is like the heat from a furnace mouth. . . . We must not either try to explain them away or to yield for one moment to the idea that, because it comes in the Bible, all this vindictive hatred must somehow be good and pious. . . . We should be wicked if we in any way condoned or approved it.[2]

Commentators generally seem to make the point less fiercely, but usually see these psalms as somehow second-class spiritually. Churches that use these psalms liturgically have in recent times also tended to delete the offensive passages. In the Church of England, which encourages worshippers to recite the whole Psalter over the course of a month, the 1928 prayer book and the 1980 Alternative Service Book bracketed many of the uncomfortable passages. Monastic orders are expected to get through the Psalter much more quickly, but they too have been encouraged to leave out the awkward verses since Vatican II.

In this short chapter I do not propose to do anything original. I want, first, to present some of the classic responses to the imprecatory psalms from the evangelical tradition, then to review a little more fully the response of a modern Catholic and, briefly, that of a Presbyterian, neither of whom I suspect would subscribe to an evangelical doctrine of Scripture. I set out these views in the hope that we shall see the issues more clearly.

---

[1] First read at a Tyndale Fellowship Old Testament group in Cambridge c. 1997; not previously published.
[2] C. S. Lewis, *Reflections on the Psalms* (London: Collins, 1961), 23–25.

Classic Responses to the Imprecatory Psalms

In reviewing commentaries, I decided to begin with John Calvin, whose exposition of the Psalms is the oldest Protestant commentary accessible to me. He does not seem to have a problem with the attitudes of the psalmist. He holds that their sentiments are inspired by God and testify to their fervor for God. Consider this comment on Psalm 139:21–22:

> Do I not hate them that hate thee, O Lord?
>   And do I not loathe them that rise up against thee?
> I hate them with perfect hatred:
> I count them my enemies.

The love of godliness thrives not sufficiently in our hearts, unless it engender such a hatred of wickedness as David speaks of here. . . .

For whosoever winks at wicked deeds, and encourages them by his silence, is a falsehearted betrayer of God's cause, who committeth to all of us the defence of his righteousness. . . .

The pursuit of our own welfare, estimation, and ease, so carry us away, that we hesitate not to undertake any contest whenever any man offends us; but in maintaining God's glory we are timorous and heartless. According, therefore, as every one of us is devoted to self, and consults his own interests, so no other cause moves us to debates, quarrellings, frays, and battles, but to revenge our own injuries. But if the majesty of God be impeached, no man stirs himself. But if a zeal of God thrive in us, it will shew itself by this stoutheartedness, when we had rather be at deadly feud with the wicked and the despisers of God, than be alienated from God for their sakes.[3]

Calvin is barely fazed by the intemperate curses of Psalm 109, usually regarded as the worst of the imprecatory psalms. He takes these curses as uttered by David himself, not by his enemies, a move that at least draws the sting of this psalm. Calvin admits that it

---

[3] John Calvin, *A Commentary on the Psalms of David* (Oxford: Tegg, 1840), 3:427–28.

would be possible to curse one's enemies out of straight hate, but he thinks that in this case, "seeing David has not spoken but by the moving of the Holy Ghost, this cursing is to be taken exactly as if God himself should thunder out of his heavenly throne."[4]

Soon thereafter he goes on to suggest that we must be more careful than David in invoking God's judgment on enemies, lest it be God's purpose to bring them to repentance. We should only curse those beyond hope of redemption.

> Only let the faithful restrain themselves in meekness, that the casting down of their heart may ascend into the sight of God. And as it is not given to us to discern the elect from the reprobate, we must learn to wish well to all such as trouble us; to desire the salvation of all mankind; yea, and to be careful for every individual person. And yet meanwhile this will be no hindrance, if our minds are pure and composed, but that we may freely appeal to God's judgment, that he should destroy all that are past hope of recovery.[5]

Calvin's hesitation about the propriety of praying these psalms did of course grow. If we should not use them except on those beyond repentance, should we ever use them? Is any living person ever beyond hope of return to God? It thus seems wiser to play it safe and exclude the use of imprecations altogether. To be frank, they are sub-Christian. Whatever the psalmists' other insights, they had not the benefit of our Lord's teaching on forgiveness, and so let us be open about their inadequacies. This is the line taken in A. F. Kirkpatrick's excellent commentary and by many others. Let him speak for himself:

> We are startled to find the most lofty and spiritual meditations interrupted by passionate prayers for vengeance upon enemies, or ending in triumphant exultation at their destruction. How, we ask can such utterances be part of a divine revelation? How

---

[4] Ibid., 3:127.
[5] Ibid.

can the men who penned them have been in any sense inspired by the Holy Spirit?[6]

According to Kirkpatrick these psalms

> must be viewed as belonging to the dispensation of the Old Testament; they must be estimated from the standpoint of the Law, which was based upon the rule of retaliation, and not of the Gospel, which is animated by the principle of love; they belong to the spirit of Elijah, not of Christ; they use the language of the age which was taught to love its neighbour and hate its enemy.[7]

Kirkpatrick recognizes some mitigating factors. The psalmists' vindictiveness sprang from a zeal for God. It was less evil to pray for God to punish one's enemies than to take the law into one's own hands and wreak unbridled revenge on them. It reflects a belief that God ought to be seen to rule the world. Desire for retribution in the present age was understandable in an era that had no conception of the final judgment. The Old Testament had not learned "to distinguish between the evil man and evil: to love the sinner while we hate the sin."[8]

But admitting these points does not justify our using these psalms.

> These utterances then belong to the spirit of the O.T. and not the N.T., and by it they must be judged. They belong to the age in which the martyr's dying prayer was not, "Lord, lay not this sin to their charge" (Acts vii. 60), but "Jehovah look upon it, and require it" (2 Chron. xxiv. 22). It is impossible that such language should be repeated in its old and literal sense by any follower of Him Who has bidden us to love our enemies and pray for them that persecute us.[9]

---

[6] A. F. Kirkpatrick, *The Book of Psalms* (Cambridge: Cambridge University Press, 1902), lxxxviii–lxxxix.
[7] Ibid., lxxxix.
[8] Ibid., xcii.
[9] Ibid., xciii.

Derek Kidner adopts a rather similar approach to Kirkpatrick, though he is somewhat more nuanced in his critique of the Old Testament. Like Kirkpatrick he says Christians have a different understanding of the gospel and the life to come, which must modify their approach to these psalms. "To get fully in tune with the psalmists on this issue we should have to suspend our consciousness of having a gospel to impart (which affects our attitude to fellow-sinners) and our assurance of a final righting of wrongs (which affects our attitude to present anomalies)."[10]

Kidner argues that David, as known from the books of Samuel, was not a vindictive man, and therefore the psalms attributed to him should not be taken in this sense.[11] Kidner goes on to urge that we recognize the language as hyperbole giving an insight into "the desperation that produced them."[12] The New Testament introduces a perspective on judgment more comprehensive and terrifying than the psalmists'. It also quotes Psalms 69 and 109 as predictions of the judgment that befell Judas. There are occasional prayers in the New Testament for judgment on enemies of the gospel. "But," says Kidner, "the fewness of these prayers or oracles of judgment, and the absence of bitterness, are proof enough of the new thing that has happened."[13] He explains:

> Between our day and theirs, our calling and theirs, stands the cross. We are ministers of reconciliation, and this is a day of good tidings.
>
> To the question, Can a Christian use these cries for vengeance as his own? The short answer must surely be No; no more than he should echo the curses of Jeremiah or the protests of Job. He may of course translate them into affirmations of

---

[10] Derek Kidner, *Psalms 1–72* (Leicester: Inter-Varsity, 1973), 26.

[11] Ibid., 26–27. This seems quite a weak argument, though it is also used by my father in *The Enigma of Evil: Can We Believe in the Goodness of God?* (Guildford: Eagle, 1994), 174–75. It presupposes that the psalms of David were by David of course, but some of the imprecatory psalms are attributed to authors other than David. It also assumes that the books of Samuel portray David's character as generous, whereas in later life he appears quite ruthless. For these reasons it would be better to allow the psalms to speak for themselves, and if one accepts their Davidic origin, to allow them to be the primary witness to David's inner character.

[12] Kidner, *Psalms 1–72*, 27–28.

[13] Ibid., 31.

God's judgment, and into denunciations of "the spiritual hosts of wickedness" which are the real enemy.[14]

If Derek Kidner is close to Kirkpatrick, Alec Motyer stands closer to Calvin. He offers three reasons why it is unsatisfactory to reject the imprecatory psalms simply as Old Testament morality. (1) Similar sentiments are expressed in the New Testament. If there is a problem, it is a biblical problem, not simply an Old Testament problem. (2) The Old Testament, like the New, urges love, God's hatred of violence, the duty of returning good for evil, and the rejection of vengeance. (3) In almost every case the imprecation that we find objectionable sits alongside a spirituality we would envy, as in Psalm 139. He further observes that these psalms are just prayers: the psalmists are not asserting the right to take revenge themselves, as many moderns do. And, finally, Motyer notes that our prayers for the second coming or for God's intervention on behalf of others are in fact requesting something similar to the psalmists, but without their lurid language. "Their prayers shock us because of their realism."[15]

Zenger's Approach to the Imprecatory Psalms

Having looked at some relatively cursory treatments of the imprecatory psalms, I should like now to sum up the arguments of Erich Zenger in his book *A God of Vengeance? Understanding the Psalms of Divine Wrath*. Originally published in Germany in 1994, it is I think the most powerful modern discussion of the issues involved. Zenger is known in Germany as a commentator on the Psalms who employed redaction and canonical criticism to elucidate their meaning. His theories of Pentateuchal criticism also appear to be widely respected. He was also a Benedictine monk accustomed to chanting the whole Psalter in the course of the daily offices. But he was infuriated by liturgical reforms in

---

[14] Ibid., 32.
[15] J. Alec Motyer, "The Psalms," in *New Bible Commentary*, ed. Gordon J. Wenham, J. Alec Motyer, Donald A. Carson, and R. T. France (Leicester: Inter-Varsity, 1994), 488.

the church, which have "in an act of magisterial barbarism . . . destroyed the poetic form of some psalms by simply eliminating individual verses."[16] In his book he argues that such censorship is quite unnecessary and deprives the church of a vital resource in the world of violence in which we live. The passages in question are a bulwark against despair and can sustain us in situations that could break us.

Zenger argues that this censorship of the First Testament, as he calls the Old Testament, reflects a residual Marcionism in Christian theology that very often is at least couched in anti-Jewish language, if not anti-Semitic or Nazi ideology. He points out that some of the "nicest" psalms, for example Psalms 8 and 23, express violence against enemies. He examines in detail the seven "worst" imprecatory psalms, three of which have been expunged entirely from the Liturgy of the Hours. Zenger then argues that a belief in divine judgment is essential in a world where there is much suffering, oppression, and justice. If we do not believe in this judgment, we have no gospel to offer to the suffering world. These psalms awaken our consciences to the anguish of those who suffer. They serve to wake us from the dreadful passivity that has overtaken the comfortable churches of the Western world. They make us long for the coming of the kingdom in power and justice.

Having sketched the outline of his argument, I shall now go through it a little more fully, quoting or paraphrasing some of his most telling passages at length.

Zenger begins by demonstrating how prevalent are violent images in the Psalter, so that we cannot adequately deal with the problem by simply cutting out a few verses here or there. Not only Psalms 8:1–4, 23:5, and 145:20 are awkward, but the very psalms that frame the Psalter, define its theme, and set its tone contain this note. Psalm 1 includes the lines:

---

[16] Erich Zenger, *A God of Vengeance? Understanding the Psalms of Divine Wrath*, trans. Linda M. Maloney (Louisville: Westminster John Knox, 1996), viii.

> The wicked are not so,
>> but are like chaff that the wind drives away. . . .
>
> the way of the wicked will perish. (vv. 4, 6)

Psalm 2 speaks of the divine Son breaking them with a rod of iron and dashing them in pieces like a potter's vessel (v. 9). At the other end of the Psalter there is rejoicing that the faithful will

> execute vengeance on the nations
>> and punishments on the peoples. (149:7)

Zenger agrees with Norbert Lohfink that the dominant theme of the Psalter is the relationship between the one praying and his enemies.[17]

Zenger then amasses quotations from famous Protestant and Catholic commentators who have argued that the imprecatory psalms are sub-Christian and must no longer be used. He also mentions the objections of pastors and psychologists. He quotes German psychologist Franz Buggle, who argues that modern people reject the Bible not because God is pictured as creating the world in seven days, but because of his unethical behavior. In the eyes of the unbeliever the biblical God behaves much worse than many human beings, reflecting an outdated morality that views suffering as the punishment for sin. This is coupled with a horror of the suffering and evil in the world, which seems incompatible with the Christian assertion that there is a loving and omniscient God who governs his creation.[18]

In chapter 2 of *A God of Vengeance?* Zenger analyzes and interprets seven psalms that bear on this question of violence and God: Psalms 12, 44, 58, 83, 109, 137, 139. It is 58, 83, and 109 that have been omitted from the Liturgy of the Hours. Zenger's exegesis is careful, thorough, and sensible. Here I should simply

---

[17] Ibid., 12.
[18] Franz Buggle, *Denn sie wissen nicht, was sie glauben* (Reinbek, 1992), 79–80, quoted in Zenger, *God of Vengeance?*, 22–23.

like to quote his initial plea for taking these texts seriously if we are to understand them. He pleads for dialogue with these violent psalms, and true dialogue involves taking the other side seriously. We must understand them before we can express our disagreement. These psalms may seem very foreign to us on first acquaintance, but we need to ask ourselves why that is so. Could it be something in us that makes it difficult for us to appreciate their standpoint? Such honest introspection could lead to a lively struggle with the text and even to seeing them as friends, not as enemies. Indeed that could lead to a change in our perspectives.

> Without jumping into the conversation too quickly, without shoving them aside in know-it-all fashion, without expressing judgment out of a sense of Christian superiority, we need to try to understand these texts in their historical context, their linguistic shape, and their theological passion. That is the first task.[19]

It is in chapter 3, "Toward a Hermeneutic of the Psalms of Enmity and Vengeance," that Zenger's study becomes most interesting. He states that he is interested in neither defending the Psalms just because they are revelation nor trying to put them at the center of worship. He wants to free them from being misunderstood because of our erroneous theology. "My concern is . . . to remove the misunderstandings that arise *in us* when and because we hear these psalms too much in terms of our own feelings about life" and Christian clichés.[20]

Zenger therefore begins by refocusing the Christian doctrine of judgment. Since the Middle Ages people have seen final judgment almost entirely as passing before God one by one to be judged for their own sins. They have lost sight of the idea that the last judgment is the time when all the injustice and suffering of the world will be ended, which is why the early church prayed so fervently for the second coming.

Zenger says, "Probably the most important thing we can

[19] Zenger, *God of Vengeance?*, 25.
[20] Ibid., 63.

say about God is that the world and history belong to *God*, and it is *God* who has the last word about history, as its 'judge.'"[21] He quotes the *Introduction to Christianity* by Joseph Ratzinger (Benedict XVI):

> Primitive Christianity, with its prayer, "Our Lord, come" (*Maranatha*), interpreted the return of Jesus as an event full of hope and joy; these early Christians yearned longingly towards it as the moment of the great fulfillment. To the Christians of the Middle Ages, on the other hand, that moment appeared as the terrifying "day of wrath" (Dies irae).[22]

According to Zenger, modern Christians have forgotten or suppressed the idea that the day of judgment is to bring justice to the victims of injustice—a day when God will restore the world to what it should be—and to confront the wicked with the reality of their sin and its consequences. This failure to bring out God's ultimate concern to right the world's wrongs has led to a preaching failure. Zenger asks whether preachers have obscured the fact that the final judgment will bring an end to injustice and liberate those who have suffered from injustice. He suggests that preachers have tended to denounce the sins of the weak while keeping quiet about the injustices perpetrated by the powerful.

> We must ask, have we in the church not often been responsible for obscuring this liberating meaning of the message about God's final judgment, because we have preached the word of judgment loudly and urgently to the weak and defenseless, while frequently our preaching has been too soft and half-hearted when directed to the powerful of this earth?[23]

The Psalms, Zenger argues, address situations where injustice cannot be righted. The sufferer is appealing to God to intervene.

---

[21] Ibid.
[22] Joseph Ratzinger, *Einführung in das Christentum* (Munich: Kösel, 1968), 271, quoted in Zenger, *God of Vengeance?*, 64.
[23] Synod of Würzburg, quoted in Zenger, *God of Vengeance?*, 65.

These cries for help are not about minor conflicts that could be resolved by greater generosity on the part of the one praying or by the exercise of love of neighbor. Rather those who pray these psalms are crying out about the injustice they suffer and are protesting about the arrogance of the violent. They are impelled by the contradiction posed by the mystery of evil and the presence of evil people in a world supposedly in God's care. This is not a trivial or selfish complaint: they are protesting not just because they are being hurt, but because God's justice, goodness, and power are at stake. These are not mere grievances about their own suffering; rather they are protests about the challenge that real wickedness poses for believers in an omnipotent God of love. The passion that drives these laments arises from a belief in God's justice that is called in question by unrestrained evil. This appeal to God for justice does not of course relieve human courts and judges from doing their best to dispense it, but it does reflect the painful reality that human justice will never be perfect, and that in many cases it is a travesty.[24]

Zenger then quotes Gottfried Bachl at length on why the message of God's judgment is good news. Bachl tells of an SS officer who commanded a squad who wiped out a whole village of some six hundred people in retaliation for the activities of the French resistance. Later this officer settled in East Germany, where he became a much respected member of the community. When eventually in 1980 he was tried and condemned to life imprisonment, he agreed to an interview, during which he repeatedly broke down in tears.

> When the reporter asked, "Why are you crying now?" he answered, "Because I have been so happy, and now it ends this way." The journalist continued, "Did you ever weep over the children, women, and men you killed that day? "No," he said. "Did it never occur to you that you had done a terrible injustice to those people?" His answer: "No, not as long as I was

---

free. Everything was quite normal. But now I often think that there must have been something wrong, that I was involved in it myself somehow, that probably the whole thing was wrong."[25]

Bachl comments that it was judgment that made this man face up to his guilt. That woke him from his happy oblivion and self-satisfaction. It was judgment that prompted him to respond as a human being who recognized what he had done. Bachl continues:

> The current of our history does not issue in justice, but in the question: Where will it happen? Will it ever appear in its true, comprehensive form. No court . . . will be adequate to the things that people . . . are doing to one another. . . . What happens in the world of humanity is from its very beginning a cry for God's judgment. And the first response to that cry that is found in the gospel, the *good* news is:
>
> The stream of events will not run on forever, over blood and victims, goodness, evil, innocence and justice. *God* will put an end to the course of history and will make clear that there is a difference between justice and injustice, and that this difference must be demonstrated. God will seek out the buried victims, the forgotten, starved children, the dishonoured women, and God will find the hidden doers of these deeds. God will gather all of them before God's eternal, holy will for the good, so that all *must* see how it stands with their lives.[26]

Zenger applies these insights to the Old Testament vision of God as Judge. They remind us that God is intensely concerned with justice in this world. To eliminate prayers that God would pour out his wrath on our enemies "would reduce the biblical God to a spectator uninterested in this world."[27] It would make God redundant, relegating him to a mere human idea—indeed an idea that has no power to criticize social ills. In truth, the language of

---

[25] Gottfried Bachl, "Das Gericht," *Christ in der Gegenwart* 45 (1993): 397, quoted in Zenger, *God of Vengeance?*, 67.

[26] Bachl, "Das Gericht," 397, quoted in Zenger, *God of Vengeance?*, 68.

[27] Zenger, *God of Vengeance?*, 73.

these psalms, with their talk of divine wrath, highlights God's hatred of injustice.

The Old Testament views history as a constant struggle between order and chaos, life and death, and these psalms represent the psalmist taking sides with order. "They are the expression of a passionate conviction that this situation contradicts what they believe and hope about the reality of God. Thus these psalms are intended to be a challenge, a calling forth of God to fight against chaos."[28]

Why do these sentiments make us so uncomfortable? Could it be, asks Zenger,

> that the directness of the challenge to God and the certainty it expresses that God must be at work in history and society form the real provocation of these psalms for a Christianity whose belief in God has exhausted its historical potential in soteriology or postponed it to an afterlife by a privatist and spiritualizing attitude?

These psalms can serve to wake us from our structural amnesia about God.[29]

Zenger goes on to list the advantages of using the imprecatory psalms, which he points out are just the strongest specimens of lament psalms:

1. They remind us of the pervasiveness of violent oppression.
2. They remind us of the distortion of the creation we live in.
3. They bring the pain of the suffering into religious life. Zenger quotes Metz, who thinks Christianity has been distorted by becoming so theological that it is no earthly good: "In the process of this theologizing Christianity lost its sensitivity to suffering . . . ; that is, it ceased to be troubled by the question of justice for innocent sufferers. In the same moment, it lost its sensitivity to time; that is, it ceased to be troubled by the question of the end of time: How long? *Maranatha!* This two-in-one loss is ordinarily not regarded as loss; instead, it

---

[28] Ibid., 74.
[29] Ibid.

is seen as a victory, the victory of theological reason . . . over the Jewish traditions in Christianity. But in my opinion it lies at the root of the present crisis of authority for Christianity." Because we have shunned these psalms, Metz holds that Christian theology has lost its sensitivity to suffering.[30]

4. Because these "psalms of enmity express sensitivity to suffering in light of the misfortune *of others* within *their own* address to God in prayer, those who pray them are inevitably faced with the question of *their own* complicity in the web of violence."[31] In other words these psalms should prompt us to ask ourselves how far we are responsible for or at least involved in structures of injustice and oppression.

Zenger points out that Jesus died on the cross reciting a lament, Psalm 22, which surely gives us warrant for using them.

As poetic prayers, the psalms of vengeance are a passionate clinging to God when everything really speaks *against* God. For that reason they can rightly be called *psalms of zeal*, to the extent that in them passion for God is aflame in the midst of the ashes of doubt about God and despair over human beings.[32]

Unfortunately "because lament has largely disappeared from our Christian prayer literature, it is not surprising that many Christians react with bewilderment to these psalms of lament and accusation."[33] Zenger comments:

Those who sing these songs sing them as a cry for change and a melody of longing for a world without tears, usually in melancholy because this world will never exist without tears. Therefore they sing them as songs of protest and struggle. All of this harmonizes as a powerful song of resistance against the

---

[30] Johannes B. Metz, *Diagnosen zur Zeit* (Düsseldorf, 1994), 84–85, quoted in Zenger, *God of Vengeance?*, 75.

[31] Zenger, *God of Vengeance?*, 76.

[32] Ibid., 79.

[33] Ibid., 78.

thin melodies that sing of a life of indifferent self-satisfaction and idyllic surrender to God.[34]

This last comment sounds like a swipe at modern Catholic worship songs, but I fear it is just as applicable to many Protestant ones.

The final chapter of Zenger's book is about reintroducing the lament genre back into Christian worship. He suggests two points in the Eucharist where lament could be helpfully incorporated. In the confession, instead of simply lamenting our sins, we could confess the suffering of the world caused by sin. The intercessions are another point where lament could be used. He advocates using even psalms like 137 in worship, perhaps with a paraphrase of the most shocking verses, so that people understand them rather than reject them. Its last lines could run:

> O daughter Babylon, you devastator!
> > Happy the one who brings you to judgment
> > because of what you have done to us!
> Happy the one who seizes you
> > and puts an end to your rule forever![35]

As an Anglican, I think we could more often use the old litany, which comes near to being a lament. But whatever we decide to do, I agree with Zenger when he quotes Gottfried Bitter: "I desire for myself and our congregations a revival of the prayer lament— against our obvious apathy and against a dreaded passivity on the part of God, in face of our disappointment with this God and our own powerless protest."[36]

McCann's View of the Imprecatory Psalms

I want to conclude this chapter by drawing attention to another way in which we could use the imprecatory psalms. It comes

---

[34] Ibid., 79–80.
[35] Ibid., 91.
[36] Gottfried Bitter, *Lebendiges Zeugnis* 39 (1984): 60, quoted in Zenger, *God of Vengeance?*, 90.

from Clinton McCann's *Theological Introduction to the Book of the Psalms*, a work that is too little known but, I think, makes the best case for the Psalms, despite a little political correctness. Chapter 7 is entitled "Prayer and Activity: Vengeance, Catharsis, and Compassion" and is devoted to discussing Psalms 82, 109, and 137. In particular, McCann comments:

> Psalm 109 not only tells it like it is with us, but also tells how it is with the world. The psalmist had been victimized; and when persons become victims, they are bound to react with rage. . . . When persons are treated unjustly, we can expect them to lash out; we can expect them to express vehemently the desire for an end to the violence that has made them a victim.[37]

McCann, contrary to Zenger, holds that Psalm 109:6–19 represents the psalmist's sentiments, not his enemies'. He writes:

> Psalm 109 is an eloquent affirmation of God's compassion for the poor and needy, and this affirmation is the basis of the psalmist's appeal. . . . God's fundamental character is to stand with and for the poor and needy. To be instructed by Psalm 109 is to take our stand with God and with the poor and needy.
>
> To be sure, there is nothing morally inferior or "un-Christian" about this psalm as instruction. But what about Psalm 109 as a prayer? Can it be a Christian prayer? Can it be our prayer? In discussions of Psalm 109 in church groups, people have frequently told me that they have never been *that* angry. I believe them. Most persons who read this book have never been so completely victimized as the psalmist of Psalm 109. But if this means that Psalm 109 cannot be our prayer ourselves, can it then be our prayer for others? In speaking the psalmic prayers, Mays[38] suggests this possibility in a moving and compelling way:

---

[37] J. Clinton McCann Jr., *A Theological Introduction to the Book of Psalms* (Nashville: Abingdon Press, 1993), 114.

[38] James Mays, lecture, April 2, 1991.

Could the use of these prayers remind us and bind us to all those in the worldwide Church who are suffering in faith and for faith? All may be well in our place. There may be no trouble for the present that corresponds to the tribulations described in the Psalms, but do we need to do more than call the roll of such places as El Salvador, South Africa, and China to remember that there are sisters and brothers whose trials could be given voice in our recitation of the Psalms? The old Church believed that it was all the martyrs who prayed in their praying the psalmic prayers.

Would it be possible to say them for the sake of and in the name of fellow Christians known to us? We do make intercessions for them, but perhaps these psalms can help us do more than simply, prayerfully wish grace and help for them, help us to find words to represent their hurt, alienation, failure and discouragement. . . .

The apostle said that "If one member suffers, all suffer together" (1 Cor 12:26), and he also said "Bear one another's burdens" (Gal 6:2). Can these prayers become a way of doing that?

McCann replies, "Yes they can. Psalm 109 teaches us and calls us to care for other persons, to bear one another's burdens, to stand in solidarity and in suffering with the poor and needy, because God 'stands at the right hand of the needy, to save them from those who would condemn them to death.'" (v. 31).[39]

[39] McCann, *Theological Introduction to the Book of Psalms*, 116–17.

CHAPTER 7

Psalm 103:
The Song of Steadfast Love[1]

"A text out of context is a pretext," preachers are often warned. You can justify almost anything from the Bible by taking texts out of context: the prosperity gospel, murder, even atheism. Establishing the context of remarks in the Bible is a prerequisite for understanding what they teach. So in reading Psalm 103, we need to contextualize it; otherwise we may distort its message.

But with the Psalms we are on particularly tricky ground, as a quick survey of commentaries will show. Commentators before the nineteenth century accepted the psalm titles as genuine; so this one with its heading, "A psalm of David," was ascribed to him. By the end of the nineteenth century most commentators rejected the authenticity of the titles and dated most of the psalms later than David. For example, Charles Briggs[2] claimed that this psalm comes from the late Greek period, something like 200 BC, thus eight centuries after David.

Twentieth-century scholarship introduced a fundamental shift in contextualizing the psalms. Whereas earlier commentators read the psalms as religious poems of the devout in ancient Israel, whether David or some unknown later writer, in the twentieth century the psalms came to be seen as essentially cultic, that is, composed for singing in the temple of Jerusalem. John Eaton, one of the most uplifting commentators on the Psalms, thinks that Psalm 103 was written for use in the autumn festival of tabernacles.[3]

---

[1] A Bible exposition at Trinity College, Bristol, on February 26, 2010; not previously published.
[2] Charles A. Briggs, *A Critical and Exegetical Commentary on the Book of Psalms* (Edinburgh: T&T Clark, 1906), 2:324.
[3] John H. Eaton, *The Psalms* (London: T&T Clark, 2003), 358.

But the end of the century saw yet another shift in contextualizing the psalms. Each psalm should be read in the context of the whole Psalter. This canonical approach has been the most innovative and, in my view, the least speculative of all critical readings. After all, we do have the Psalter as a book. It is obviously carefully arranged in five books. And the links between adjacent psalms are often unmistakable, so that it is obvious that the psalms are meant to be read or recited in sequence. For the editors of the Psalter, it may be presumed that the titles were also significant.

So in this exposition of Psalm 103, I want to read it as the editors of the Psalter understood it. This will involve looking at its place in the Psalter, its connections with other psalms (especially those close to it), and its title.

The first thing to note is that it begins and ends with the exhortation, "Bless the LORD, O my soul." This links Psalm 103 to the immediately following Psalm 104, which also begins and ends with those words. Psalm 104 praises the perfection of God's creation; it is a poetic paraphrase of Genesis 1. Psalm 105 sums up the story of Israel from the patriarchs to the exodus. And, finally, Psalm 106 concludes book 4 of the Psalter by recounting Israel's sins in the wilderness, that is, the stories found in Exodus to Deuteronomy. In other words, Psalms 104 to 106 are a poetic recapitulation of the Pentateuch, Genesis to Deuteronomy.

But as I have already noted, Psalm 103 is linked to Psalm 104 by its opening and closing refrain, "Bless the LORD, O my soul." It therefore serves as a prelude to the summary of the Pentateuch in the following three psalms. Why should it preface these psalms in this way? Without Psalm 103, the next three psalms make a very gloomy impression. All God's generosity displayed in creation (Psalm 104) and redemption, that is, the call of Abraham and the exodus from Egypt—what did it lead to? How did Israel respond? By one act of rebellion after another, by sin after sin, by idolatry, by worshipping Baal in the wilderness, by mixing with the nations, by sacrificing their children to Canaanite gods, and so on. Consequently, Psalm 106 says,

> Then the anger of the LORD was kindled against his people,
>> and he abhorred his heritage;
> he gave them into the hand of the nations,
>> so that those who hated them ruled over them. (vv. 40–41)

These comments reflect the situation when the Psalter was edited. Israel was in exile in Babylon, suffering for her sins. Was there still hope for her? The plaintive plea with which the psalm ends leaves one wondering.

> Save us, O LORD our God,
>> and gather us from among the nations,
> that we may give thanks to your holy name
>> and glory in your praise. (Ps. 106:47)

The previous verses give some hope (see vv. 44–46). But what really clarifies its meaning is the setting of Psalm 103 before the gloomy sequence of Psalms 104 to 106. Psalm 103 celebrates God's steadfast love, which was demonstrated in God's pardoning of two of the nation's greatest sins: the golden calf and David's adultery. If Moses and David experienced God's mercy so many years ago, may not exiled Israel hope for another act of divine mercy?

Looking at the psalms that precede 103 deepens this conviction. As I have mentioned, the Psalter is divided into five books, like the Pentateuch. The first two books, Psalms 1–41, 42–72, end with a very upbeat psalm, David's prayer for Solomon.

> May he have dominion from sea to sea,
>> and from the River to the ends of the earth!
> May desert tribes bow down before him,
>> and his enemies lick the dust!
> May the kings of Tarshish and of the coastlands
>> render him tribute;
> may the kings of Sheba and Seba
>> bring gifts!
> May all kings fall down before him,
>> all nations serve him! (Ps. 72:8–11)

Solomon of course did not live up to his father's hopes, either militarily or socially. His father prayed,

> For he delivers the needy when he calls,
>> the poor and him who has no helper.
> He has pity on the weak and the needy,
>> and saves the lives of the needy.
> From oppression and violence he redeems their life,
>> and precious is their blood in his sight. (vv. 12–14)

But Solomon's reign was marked by quite oppressive policies (see 1 Kings 12:1–15).

Eventually the great empire of David fell apart, leaving the little kingdom of Judah at the mercy of the Babylonians. They conquered Jerusalem and deposed the Davidic king. This seemed to disprove the promises given to David that there would always be one of his descendants on the throne in Jerusalem. So book 3 of the Psalter ends with this plea to God:

> But now you have cast off and rejected;
>> you are full of wrath against your anointed.
> You have renounced the covenant with your servant;
>> you have defiled his crown in the dust.
> You have breached all his walls;
>> you have laid his strongholds in ruins.
> All who pass by plunder him;
>> he has become the scorn of his neighbors.
> You have exalted the right hand of his foes;
>> you have made all his enemies rejoice.
> You have also turned back the edge of his sword,
>> and you have not made him stand in battle.
> You have made his splendor to cease
>> and cast his throne to the ground.
> You have cut short the days of his youth;
>> you have covered him with shame.   *Selah*

> How long, O LORD? Will you hide yourself forever?
>> How long will your wrath burn like fire?

Remember how short my time is!
> For what vanity you have created all the children of man!
What man can live and never see death?
> Who can deliver his soul from the power of Sheol?   *Selah*

Lord, where is your steadfast love of old,
> which by your faithfulness you swore to David? (Ps. 89:38–49)

Book 4, that is Psalms 90–106, is an answer to this plea. Three convictions inform this plea. First, the unchangeability and eternity of God. The book begins:

Book Four
A PRAYER OF MOSES, THE MAN OF GOD.

Lord, you have been our dwelling place
> in all generations.
Before the mountains were brought forth,
> or ever you had formed the earth and the world,
> from everlasting to everlasting you are God.

You return man to dust
> and say, "Return, O children of man!"
For a thousand years in your sight
> are but as yesterday when it is past,
> or as a watch in the night. (Ps. 90:1–4)

This theme is central to Psalm 103, for example, verse 17: "The steadfast love of the LORD is from everlasting to everlasting."

The second conviction is that God reigns, that God is king, that he is sovereign. Several psalms from 93 to 99 contain the refrain "The LORD reigns." This too comes out in our psalm.

The LORD has established his throne in the heavens,
> and his kingdom rules over all. (Ps. 103:19)

But the third and most important conviction is "the steadfast love of God." This is the key word in our psalm, as seen in verse 17: "The steadfast love of the LORD is from everlasting to everlasting." The word in Hebrew is *hesed*. It is translated "steadfast love" by the RSV and its successor translations, "mercy" in the KJV and the Church of England prayer book, and "love" in the NIV. The NLT is inconsistent, offering a variety of translations: "love," "unfailing love," "faithful love." I hope by the end of this exposition you will be able to say which translation of *hesed* best captures the sense in this psalm.

It is indeed a favorite word of the psalmists, occurring 127 times in the Psalter out of 245 times in the whole Old Testament. Since the Psalms constitute less than 8 percent of the Old Testament, yet contain more than half the uses of *hesed*, you can see how significant it is in the theology of the Psalms. In Psalm 103 it occurs four times: in verses 4, 8, 11, and 17. So central is *hesed* to this psalm that one commentator[4] has dubbed it "the Song of Songs of Grace."

So let us turn to the psalm to see if we can unpack the idea of *hesed* more fully. Psalm 103 may be divided into 5 parts:

- Verses 1–5. The psalmist calls on his whole being to thank God for saving him from sickness that could have killed him.
- Verses 6–10. The psalmist's experience echoes that of Moses and Israel in the wilderness.
- Verses 11–14. God's pardoning mercy is amazing in its comprehensiveness.
- Verses 15–18. Human life is short and transitory, but God's *hesed* is eternal and guarantees the future of the descendants of those who fear him.
- Verses 19–22. The psalmist calls all creation to praise God.

We should note that the psalm begins with summoning "my soul," one individual, to praise God: "Bless the LORD, O my soul." Then it moves into the plural: "He does not deal with us according to our sins" (v. 10);

---

[4] Klaus Seybold, *Die Psalmen* (Tübingen: Mohr, 1996), 402.

He knows our frame;
>he remembers that we are dust. (v. 14)

Finally, the psalmist summons the whole cosmos to praise God with him: the angels, his hosts—that is, other heavenly beings, including the sun, moon, and stars—and all his created works. The hymn "Praise My Soul the King of Heaven" sums up this conclusion well.

Angels, help us to adore him,
>ye behold him face to face,
Sun and moon, bow down before him,
>dwellers all in time and space.

But who is the psalmist who sums up his experience and invites the whole of creation to praise God for it? Most commentaries do not bother to investigate this question. Yet the heading of the psalm tells us who the compilers of the Psalter thought responsible. This is one of only three psalms in book 4 ascribed to a particular author. Most of the psalms in book 4 are anonymous, just two are ascribed to David, and one belongs to Moses. So evidently the title "Of David" is significant and should be borne in mind as we read the psalm. We should ask ourselves, what do we know of David's life that might illuminate the words of this psalm? Let us look more carefully at this psalm.

Bless the LORD, O my soul,
>and all that is within me,
>bless his holy name! (Ps. 103:1)

David begins by addressing himself and urging his soul to praise God—to praise him with "all that is within me," literally "my inwards." In biblical psychology, one's thoughts, decisions, and emotions are associated with the heart, kidneys, and intestines, deep down inside the person. So David is urging himself, and us when we pray the psalm, to give ourselves entirely to God in worship. He warns his soul, "forget not all his benefits" (v. 2). It is far too easy to forget what God has done for us, as Deuteronomy often warns Israel. Beware lest you forget the Lord your God by not keeping his commandments. We see our cup half empty rather than half full, but the hymn reminds us,

> Count your blessings, name them one by one,
> and it will surprise you what the Lord has done.

And that is just what David does: he lists five things God has done for him. God has forgiven David's iniquity, healed him, saved him from death, shown him *hesed* and compassion, and renewed his strength like the eagle's (vv. 3–5).

It seems likely that all these blessings are seen as arising from the first. The forgiveness of David's sin led to his healing from some complaint that he thought might bring his death. God redeemed his life from "the pit," which is Sheol, or the under-world to which the unrighteous descend when they die. Though the Old Testament recognizes that not all sickness and death are due to the sin of the individual sufferer, there is often a connec-tion, and many a psalm draws attention to the possibility. The Old Testament does not mention an occasion when David was at death's door and recovered, but it does of course mention his sins, especially his adultery with Bathsheba and the elimination of her husband. For this the prophet Nathan told David that he deserved to die. But David's penitence led to his forgiveness, so that he did not die. The ascription of the psalm to David may suggest that the psalm alludes to this experience of forgiveness.

But there is no mistaking the allusion in verses 6–10. "He made known his ways to Moses" (v. 7) leads us straight to Exodus 33:13, where Moses prays, "Show me now your ways." What is Exodus 33 all about? It comes right in the middle of the story of the golden calf. While Moses has been on Mount Sinai receiving the Ten Commandments and other laws, the people of Israel under the guidance of Aaron have made a gold-plated image of a calf and started to worship it. They say, "These are your gods, O Israel, who brought you up out of the land of Egypt" (Ex. 32:8). A more blatant breaking of the first two commandments could hardly be imagined. God is angry and so is Moses. Coming down the mountain and discovering what is happening, Moses smashes the tablets on which the commandments are written, thereby symbolizing the smashing of the covenant that this idolatry has caused.

God threatens to destroy the whole nation of Israel except for Moses, with whom he will make a new start. He will make Moses's descendants into a great nation, instead of the descendants of Abraham. After a passionate prayer from Moses, God relents, but says he will not accompany Israel into the Promised Land. He will send his angel instead. Further mourning by the people and further intercession by Moses prompt God to declare that he will go with Israel after all, and he will renew the covenant with them (Ex. 32:9–33:23). So Moses prepares two new stone tablets for the commandments to be written on, climbs Mount Sinai again, and hears one of the most significant theological statements in the Bible:

> The LORD descended in the cloud and stood with him there, and proclaimed the name of the LORD. The LORD passed before him and proclaimed, "The LORD, the LORD, a God merciful and gracious, slow to anger, and abounding in steadfast love and faithfulness, keeping steadfast love for thousands, forgiving iniquity and transgression and sin, but who will by no means clear the guilty, visiting the iniquity of the fathers on the children and the children's children, to the third and the fourth generation."
> (Ex. 34:5–7)

It is some of these divine words from Sinai that Psalm 103 quotes in verse 8. One might say that Exodus 34:5–7 reveals God's character definitively as far as the Old Testament is concerned. It is quoted in two other psalms, 86 and 145, and in the prophets Joel and Jonah.[5] It is alluded to in many other passages, most

---

[5] Ps. 86:15; 145:8; Joel 2:13; Jonah 4:2.

obviously when steadfast love is linked to another term from Exodus, such as *faithfulness* or *abounding*. But it could be that anywhere *hesed* steadfast love is mentioned, Exodus 34 is ringing in the background. Certainly Exodus 32–34 demonstrates more clearly than anywhere else what *hesed* involves. It speaks of a God who is prepared to forgive the gravest of sins in response to prayer and penitence.

Psalm 103 adds further reflection. God will not always chide (v. 9), that is, he is not one to perpetuate his legal claim against sinners. The next line repeats this sentiment: "Nor will he keep his anger forever"; or more exactly, he will not bear a grudge.

In the next few verses we have a variety of words for sin: "iniquities," "sins," and "transgressions," all terms that occur in Exodus 34:7–9. But whatever their character, God has put them as far from the psalmist as possible: "as high as the heavens are above the earth, . . . as far as the east is from the west" (Ps. 103:11–12). Micah uses another vivid image of the way God deals with sin in his reflection on Exodus 34:7–9.

> Who is a God like you, pardoning iniquity
>   and passing over transgression
>   for the remnant of his inheritance?
> He does not retain his anger forever,
>   because he delights in steadfast love.
> He will again have compassion on us;
>   he will tread our iniquities underfoot.
> You will cast all our sins
>   into the depths of the sea.
> You will show faithfulness to Jacob
>   and steadfast love to Abraham,
> as you have sworn to our fathers
>   from the days of old. (Mic. 7:18–20)

But notice that this promise of unlimited forgiveness is not without a condition. Three times Psalm 103 contains the phrase "those who fear him":

- "His steadfast love [is] toward those who fear him" (v. 11).
- His "compassion [is] to those who fear him" (v. 13).
- "The steadfast love of the LORD is from everlasting to everlasting on those who fear him" (v. 17).

Only those who fear God may claim this forgiveness.

What does it mean to fear God? The fear of God describes the fundamental attitude of the righteous. "The fear of the LORD is the beginning of wisdom" (Ps. 111:10). On the other hand, the wicked are those who have no fear of God (Ps. 36:1). The fear of God involves reverence, devotion, and obedience to God. As Psalm 112:1 puts it,

> Blessed is the man who fears the LORD,
>   who greatly delights in his commandments!

The parallel between the two lines shows that one aspect of fearing God is delighting in his commandments. In the golden calf story the promise of divine forgiveness and God's continuing presence with Israel is followed by the words, "Observe what I command you this day" (Ex. 34:11).

But experience shows how difficult this is. "We are dust" (Ps. 103:14). "As for man, his days are like grass" (v. 15), here today and gone tomorrow. By contrast, God's steadfast love is eternal. His saving power extends to children's children (v. 17). This is what Moses experienced in the wilderness. He appealed to God's promises to Abraham to persuade God not to destroy Israel (Ex. 32:13). David too was promised an eternal dynasty by God: "My steadfast love I will keep for him forever" (Ps. 89:28). Now David, speaking in Psalm 103, reaffirms his faith that God will keep his promises to children's children. This is a reaffirmation of the promises to the Davidic house. The Psalter was compiled during the exile or postexilic era, when there was no Davidic king. In that context this verse must be understood as a promise of the restoration of the Davidic house, of a new Davidic king. It must be understood of the coming of the Messiah.

Thus Psalm 103 brings a message of hope to a downcast nation, which had lost its independence and monarchy, and was dispersed throughout the Middle East—some in Babylon, others in Assyria, some in Palestine, some even in Egypt. The prophets had told them that this dispersal was their fault; it was because of the people's sin. Could they be forgiven? This psalm, among others, gives hope and reassurance. God forgave the sinful David. In the time of Moses he pardoned the whole nation. God has not changed.

> The LORD has established his throne in the heavens,
>   and his kingdom rules over all. (v. 19)

So God can again restore the Davidic line. He can again restore the nation's identity—if they

> keep his covenant
>   and remember to do his commandments. (v. 18)

It is this confidence in God's steadfast love that prompts the final outburst, when the whole universe is told to bless the Lord.

> Bless the LORD, O you his angels,
>   you mighty ones who do his word,
>   obeying the voice of his word!
> Bless the LORD, all his hosts,
>   his ministers, who do his will!
> Bless the LORD, all his works,
>   in all places of his dominion.
> Bless the LORD, O my soul! (Ps. 103:20–22)

The same trust in God's steadfast love should energize us. The Western church today finds itself in a position similar to exiled Israel. We can look back to a glorious past, when the churches were full and Christian principles and values dominated national life. Now it is different. Church attendance continues to fall; according to recent statistics the Church of England has lost 3.5 percent of its flock in the seven years from 2003 to 2010, and the trend continues. Recent years have highlighted disgusting greed and corruption among our bankers and politicians. And many people are dismayed by the collapse of family life and acknowledge that we live in a broken society. Not long ago I attended a meeting for the supporters of CARE, a charity devoted to promoting Christian standards in our society. CARE does a wide variety of things, from running pregnancy care centers to lobbying members of Parliament about euthanasia, cloning, and other current issues. They can point to a great number of worthwhile achievements. But they have not stopped the tide of secularism and unbelief sweeping our culture.

Like the exiles in Babylon, we may be tempted to despair. But Psalm 103 gives us reason to hope. "The steadfast love of the LORD is from everlasting to everlasting." Whatever the church's sins of the past or the present, we can claim forgiveness. We can look for renewal. We can pray and expect God to restore his church and his people. Moses proved it, and so did David. The coming of Christ was yet further confirmation of these promises. So I see no reason why the modern church should not also enjoy forgiveness for its failures, if we truly repent. The offer is open to the greatest of sinners. But we must not miss the condition for experiencing that steadfast love: the promise is for "those who fear him," for "those who keep his covenant and remember to do his commandments." A church that fails to uphold a biblical ethic cannot expect to enjoy God's covenant blessings.

CHAPTER 8

The Nations in the Psalms[1]

When I blithely accepted an invitation to give a lecture on this topic, I thought it would be quite an easy topic. All you need to do is to look up the mentions of nations or peoples in the Psalter and then put the passages in some sort of logical order to build up a composite picture of the nations as they are depicted in the Psalms. But as I read the Psalms with this in mind and tried to digest what others have written on the topic, I realized there were problems I had not thought of. The nations are discussed even when the term is not used. Sometimes specific nations are mentioned, such as Egypt, Edom, or Babylon. Or their leaders are mentioned, their kings, who represent the nations. Some psalms that on the face of it appear to be addressed to Israel alone may in fact address all the nations. For example, Psalm 100 begins, "Make a joyful noise to the LORD all the earth!" (v. 1). Some scholars have argued that the Psalms should be read eschatologically and present a program for the future of Israel and the nations. These are a few of the issues raised by this topic.

But there is a more fundamental problem, one of exegetical method. Should we read the psalms as independent songs, or should we read them as parts of a collection? Is it right to allow the message in one psalm to influence our reading of the next? Or should each psalm be interpreted in isolation? Connected with this major issue is another. Should our exegesis aim to recover the sense of the original poet who composed the psalm, or should we be content to recover the sense of the psalm as it was understood by the editors of the Psalter? These issues have been hotly debated through the centuries, particularly in the last twenty or thirty years.

It is not my intention to discuss these issues in depth in this

---

[1] A lecture at Redcliffe College, Gloucester, May 12, 2010; not previously published.

chapter. Rather I shall simply state my preference for the modern canonical approach to the Psalms, which favors reading them in sequence in their present, final book form. The canonical approach does not ignore discussion of the original author's understanding of each psalm, but it holds that the most accessible and authoritative sense of a psalm is that of the Psalter's editor, a sense that is opened by reading the psalm within its wider context of surrounding psalms. This method is best demonstrated by Jean-Luc Vesco in his recent French commentary *Le psautier de David*.

So let us survey the psalms in sequence, noting where the nations are mentioned. The Psalter opens with two untitled psalms. Their anonymity is unusual in the first ninety psalms; thereafter a greater proportion of psalms appear without the authors' names. This anonymity at the beginning of the Psalter has led most commentators to recognize that Psalms 1 and 2 are introductory to the whole collection. Recent canonical critics would go further and affirm that these two psalms are programmatic: that is, that they introduce the major themes of the Psalter.

Psalm 1 introduces the fundamental choice facing everyone: are you one of the righteous or one of the wicked? The righteous meditates on the law of the Lord day and night, and everything he does will ultimately prosper, whereas the way of the wicked will perish. The psalms that follow are full of references to the conflicts between the righteous and wicked. Many are the complaints of the righteous as they suffer at the hands of the wicked. They cry out to God to save them in the laments, and when that happens they sing thanksgivings in gratitude.

The theme of conflict emerges with full vigor in Psalm 2.

> Why do the nations rage
> > and the peoples plot in vain?
> The kings of the earth set themselves,
> > and the rulers take counsel together,
> > > against the LORD and against his Anointed, saying,
> "Let us burst their bonds apart
> > and cast away their cords from us."

He who sits in the heavens laughs;
    the Lord holds them in derision.
Then he will speak to them in his wrath,
    and terrify them in his fury, saying,
"As for me, I have set my King
    on Zion, my holy hill." (vv. 1–6)

Here the nations, led by their kings, attack the God-appointed king in Jerusalem, as described in verses 1–3. Older form critics suggested that the background to this psalm was the accession of a new king in Jerusalem. The surrounding nations, who formed part of the Davidic empire, seized the opportunity of a new and inexperienced king in Jerusalem to rebel, to "burst their bonds apart and cast away their cords." Perhaps speaking through a prophet, God declares that the nations' plans will fail. Why? Because God has appointed the king of Jerusalem. More than that, God has adopted the new king at his coronation as his son. And as God's son, the new king will rule the nations surrounding Jerusalem. They may be thinking of rebelling, but they are advised,

Serve the LORD with fear,
    and rejoice with trembling. (v. 11)

This is the sort of scenario that older commentators think explains the original composition and its use. They may be right.

But how does one's understanding of the psalm change if one sees it as announcing a major strand in the Psalter's theology? How would it have been understood by the editor or editors of the Psalter, who must have lived in the postexilic era, when there was no Davidic empire, no king in Jerusalem, not even an independent Jewish state, but just a province of the Persian Empire? We could, I suppose, think this coronation psalm was preserved just for antiquarian interest, but its position at the beginning of the Psalter and the references later to the promises to the Davidic king make this unlikely. Rather it witnesses to an enduring belief among the Jews that God's promises to David are still valid and that there

will be a new David who will restore the great empire by recon-
quering the nations. Psalm 72:8 prays that the new Solomon will

> have dominion from sea to sea,
>> and from the River to the ends of the earth!

Similarly, Psalm 89:35–36 reminds God of his oath to David.

> Once for all I have sworn by my holiness;
>> I will not lie to David.
>> His offspring shall endure forever,
>> his throne as long as the sun before me.

Finally, near the end of the Psalter that promise is reaffirmed.

> The LORD swore to David a sure oath . . . .
> "If your sons keep my covenant . . . ,
> their sons also forever
>> shall sit on your throne." (Ps. 132:11–12)

This highlighting of the promises to David in an era when
there was no Davidic king shows that the editors of the Psalter
looked for their fulfillment in the future. In other words, they interpreted these psalms messianically. They looked for a new David,
who would emulate the achievements of his great forefather.

If the new David is yet to be revealed, so too must the activities
of the nations lie in the future: their raging, their plotting against
the new David, their subjugation, and their serving the Lord with
fear. Thus in a few verses the second psalm gives a sketch of the
Psalter's vision of the future relationship between the nations,
on the one hand, and Israel and Israel's God, on the other. David
Mitchell sums up the significance of Psalm 2 as follows:

> That means the ensuing collection is to be about ultimate war
> between the Yhwh's *mashiah* [anointed] and his foes, his tri-
> umph and the establishment of his universal dominion, centred
> on Zion. The combined effect of Psalms 1 and 2 together may be

that Psalm 1 foretells the triumph of the righteous divine king who meditates on Yhwh's Torah, and Psalm 2 shows him going forth to battle with its predicted outcome.[2]

More controversially, he goes on: "The two psalms together announce . . . the eschatological wars of the Lord, describing the coming events and the Yhwh-allegiance required of those who would triumph."[3]

Let us unpack these ideas more slowly. I think we can see in Psalm 2 five themes that keep recurring in the Psalter:

1. The divine choice of David as king (v. 7)
2. The choice of Jerusalem or Zion as God's dwelling place (v. 6)
3. The attack of the nations on the Davidic king in Jerusalem (vv. 1–3)
4. The defeat of the nations (vv. 8–9)
5. The invitation to the nations to serve the Lord (vv. 11–12)[4]

I shall trace these themes through the Psalter.

The next psalm, Psalm 3, is headed "A Psalm of David." For nearly two centuries psalm titles have been under critical suspicion. It is alleged that they are later additions and therefore cannot be relied on to tell us who actually wrote the psalms. I think most of the reasons cited for doubting the antiquity of the titles are weak and subjective. But whether the skeptics are right or wrong, these titles tell us who the editors of the Psalter thought wrote the psalms. And as I have already said, it is the editors' understanding of the psalms that we are trying to recapture. So canonical readers must take the headings seriously. We must hear the voice of David in those many psalms bearing the title "A Psalm of David."

---

[2] David C. Mitchell, *The Message of the Psalter: An Eschatological Programme in the Book of Psalms* (Sheffield: Sheffield Academic Press, 1997), 87.

[3] Ibid.

[4] V. 12 is a bit problematic with its advice to kiss the son, the word translated "son" being Aramaic. So it has been conjectured that the kings of the nations are being addressed in the lingua franca of the time, that is, in Aramaic. Whatever the correct reading, it is clear that the kings are being challenged to submit to both the Lord and his anointed king in Jerusalem.

But which of the five themes from Psalm 2 do we find when we read Psalm 3 this way?

Theme 3: An attack of the enemies

> O Lord, how many are my foes!
>   Many are rising against me;
> many are saying of my soul,
>   there is no salvation for him in God. (vv. 1–2)

Theme 1: God's choice of David

> But you, O Lord, are a shield about me,
>   my glory, and the lifter of my head. (v. 3)

Theme 2: God dwelling in his holy hill, Zion

> I cried aloud to the Lord,
>   and he answered me from his holy hill. (v. 4)

Theme 4: Faith that the enemies will be defeated

> For you strike all my enemies on the cheek;
>   you break the teeth of the wicked. (v. 7)

However, theme 5, the invitation to submit to God and his king, is not mentioned. Nor is it clear that the king's enemies are the nations; indeed the title, "A psalm of David, when he fled from Absalom his son" seems to rule out this interpretation. Another difference from Psalm 2 is the promise of victory. David prays for it, but it is not clearly promised as it was in the previous psalm. This uncertainty about the outcome of the conflicts between the righteous David and his wicked enemies runs through many psalms. Typically they end on a positive note, as in 3:8:

> Salvation belongs to the Lord;
>   your blessing be on your people!

But the presence of so many laments witnesses to the intensity and length of the struggle David faces.

If some of the titles identify David's enemies with other Israelites, does this mean that other nations are not his enemies? Apparently not in Psalm 7, where David appeals for God's intervention against his enemies.

> Lift yourself up against the fury of my enemies;
>   awake for me; you have appointed a judgment. (v. 6)

He continues,

> The LORD judges the peoples;
>   judge me, O LORD, according to my righteousness. (v. 8)

Kirkpatrick comments on this judgment scene: "The psalmist prays that 'the peoples' may be summoned to stand round the tribunal. It is a general summons. No distinction is made between Israel and other nations. Jehovah is exercising his judicial functions in their fullest extent as the Judge of all the earth."[5] This picture of the nations summoned to account for their deeds is developed in Psalm 9. It should be noted that Psalm 9 is deliberately linked with Psalm 7; the closing lines of Psalm 7 are echoed by the opening lines of Psalm 9. Psalm 7 ends,

> I will give the LORD the thanks due to his righteousness,
>   and I will sing praise to the name of the LORD, the Most
>   High. (v. 17)

Psalm 9 begins:

> I will give thanks to the LORD . . . .
>   I will sing praise to your name, O Most High.

This linkage justifies our seeing Psalm 9 as a commentary on the allusion to universal judgment in 7:8. Psalm 9 says:

---

[5] A. F. Kirkpatrick, *The Book of Psalms* (Cambridge: Cambridge University Press, 1902), 32.

> When my enemies turn back,
> > they stumble and perish before your presence.
> For you have maintained my just cause;
> > you have sat on the throne, giving righteous judgment.
>
> You have rebuked the nations; you have made the wicked perish;
> > you have blotted out their name forever and ever.
> The enemy came to an end in everlasting ruins;
> > their cities you rooted out;
> > the very memory of them has perished.
>
> But the LORD sits enthroned forever;
> > he has established his throne for justice,
> and he judges the world with righteousness;
> > he judges the peoples with uprightness. (Ps. 9:3–8)

Evidently David sees his present success as the result of the heavenly judgment in his favor (see vv. 3–4). From the perspective of the Psalter's editors this must have been problematic, for there was no David in their day. For them, the divine decree in the heaven still stood, promising them ultimate victory. In this way the hope first expressed in Psalm 2, that the nations will be defeated, is reaffirmed. But is this a destruction of all the nations? Surely not: it has in view the enemies of the Davidic king (9:3). It is destruction of the wicked, who parallel the nations in 9:5. It is their name that is blotted out forever and ever. These early Davidic psalms do not mention the possibility of some righteous among the nations who will escape this judgment, but in the light of the programmatic statement inviting them to serve the Lord (2:11), it cannot be ruled out.

This is clear in the great Davidic thanksgiving of Psalm 18. Here David, at the height of his success, having survived the challenge of Saul's family and subdued the surrounding nations, ascribes this success to the Lord.

> You made my enemies turn their backs to me . . . .
>
> You delivered me from strife with the people;

> you made me the head of the nations;
>> people whom I had not known served me.
> As soon as they heard of me they obeyed me;
>> foreigners came cringing to me.
> Foreigners lost heart
>> and came trembling out of their fortresses.
>
> The LORD lives, and blessed be my rock,
>> and exalted be the God of my salvation—
> the God who gave me vengeance
>> and subdued peoples under me,
> who delivered me from my enemies;
>> yes, you exalted me above those who rose against me;
>> you rescued me from the man of violence.
>
> For this I will praise you, O LORD, among the nations,
>> and sing to your name. (Ps. 18:40, 43–49)

That some nations survive the conflict is apparent from their service to David. He is their head. He is going to praise God among them (v. 49). Submission to the Davidic king is clearly the prerequisite for their salvation. Earlier in the psalm David says:

> With the merciful you show yourself merciful;
>> with the blameless man you show yourself blameless . . . .
> For you save a humble people,
>> but the haughty eyes you bring down. (18:25, 27)

It would therefore seem that these are qualities that David looked for in his subjects, including subjects from the nations (cf. Psalm 101).

But how would Psalm 18 have been understood by the later editors? Why did they include it for their contemporaries to meditate on? The very last verse shows that they believed this psalm was permanently relevant.

> Great salvation he [the LORD] brings to his king,

> and shows steadfast love to his anointed,
> to David and his offspring forever. (18:50)

Vesco sums up the message to the later readers.

> This Davidic psalm . . . comes to reassure the nation that God
> will come to deliver them from the oppression to which they are
> subject. . . . Psalm 18 is a messianic song of thanksgiving after
> the exile. The king awaited in the future is a model of justice.
> God will save him and make all the peoples submit to him. To
> a people in anguish this psalm brings hope. As he did at other
> times in theophanies God will intervene again on behalf of his
> messiah. . . . All the nations will recognise one day that there is
> no other God except Israel's.[6]

That there is hope for the nations is clear in the familiar Psalm
22. The first twenty verses describe in vivid detail the suffering of
David at the hands of his enemies. With such comments as "they
have pierced my hands and my feet" and "for my clothing they
cast lots," the Christian reader cannot but see this as a prophecy
of the crucifixion. And such a reading is quite consonant with a
canonical interpretation from postexilic times, for many of the
Davidic psalms describe the psalmist's suffering at the hands of
his enemies. And in the editors' understanding, they must describe
the suffering of the new David. What the evangelists and later
Christian readers do is to affirm that Jesus is that new David.

From verse 21 onward the mood of the psalm suddenly changes.
David's prayer has been heard (v. 24) and he declares, "You have
rescued me" (v. 21). The psalmist's vindication is cause for jubila-
tion among "the congregation," "the offspring of Jacob," that is,
among the Israelites, but not only them.

> All the ends of the earth shall remember
>   and turn to the LORD,
> and all the families of the nations

---

[6] Jean-Luc Vesco, *Le psautier de David traduit et commenté* (Paris: du Cerf, 2006), 203–4 (my trans.).

shall worship before you.
For kingship belongs to the Lord,
   and he rules over the nations. (vv. 27–28)

The psalmist sees the impact of this deliverance resounding into the future.

Posterity shall serve him;
   it shall be told of the Lord to the coming generation;
they shall come and proclaim his righteousness to a people
     yet unborn,
   that he has done it. (vv. 30–31)

Some commentators suggest that the psalm envisages "the conversion of all peoples,"[7] or at least that "all nations to earth's remotest bound, will pay homage to Jehovah."[8] If they mean that everyone from every nation will be converted, I think they are suggesting a universalism that conflicts with other passages in the Psalms, for example, 2:9 and 149:6–9. The scope of salvation may be universal: it is open to all nations. But not all nations, and certainly not every member of every nation, will accept the terms of that salvation.

Lohfink has argued that Psalm 23 does indeed represent the sentiments of such a convert. The psalmist calls God his shepherd, that is, his king. He is on his way to the temple in Jerusalem, where he hopes to dwell forever. Such a pilgrimage of the nations to Jerusalem is of course part of the prophetic vision of Isaiah, Micah, and Zechariah.

It shall come to pass in the latter days
   that the mountain of the house of the Lord
shall be established as the highest of the mountains,
   and shall be lifted up above the hills;
and all the nations shall flow to it,

---

[7] Franz Delitzsch, *Biblical Commentary on the Psalms* (1871; repr., Grand Rapids: Eerdmans, n.d.), 1:324.
[8] Kirkpatrick, *The Book of Psalms*, 122.

and many peoples shall come, and say:
"Come, let us go up to the mountain of the LORD,
    to the house of the God of Jacob,
that he may teach us his ways
    and that we may walk in his paths."
For out of Zion shall go the law,
    and the word of the LORD from Jerusalem.
He shall judge between the nations,
    and shall decide disputes for many peoples;
and they shall beat their swords into plowshares,
    and their spears into pruning hooks;
nation shall not lift up sword against nation,
    neither shall they learn war anymore.
        (Isa. 2:2–4; cf. Mic. 4:1–5; Zech. 14:16–19)

Then, according to Lohfink, we have in Psalm 24 the conditions for entry to the holy city to which the converted Gentiles must conform.

Who shall ascend the hill of the LORD?
    And who shall stand in his holy place?
He who has clean hands and a pure heart,
    who does not lift up his soul to what is false
    and does not swear deceitfully. (vv. 3–4)

If this is the logic of putting Psalms 23 and 24 after Psalm 22, it is possible that those who fear the Lord in Psalm 25:14 include Gentiles to whom God "makes known . . . his covenant." As Lohfink observes, it would be remarkable for other nations to be included in the covenant, but this is where the sequence of thought leads him. He writes, "The promise of the covenant of Israel also for the peoples, which Psalm 25 comprises, is obviously unique in the whole Hebrew Bible."[9] I remain intrigued, but unconvinced. The titles of the psalms, which must be taken seriously on a canonical reading, make it difficult to suppose that the author of Psalm 23

---

[9] Norbert Lohfink and Erich Zenger, *Der Gott Israels und die Völker* (Stuttgart: Katholisches Bibelwerk Verlag, 1994), 83 (my trans.).

could be a converted Gentile. Neither the historic David nor the eschatological David was a Gentile. And while the psalmists may well have known of the pilgrimage of the nations to Jerusalem, Psalm 24 would be an obscure reference to it.

While we could continue to work our way steadily through the Psalter, endeavoring to see how one psalm leads into the next, the constraints of space mean that we must be more selective. Psalm 33 is one of the few hymns in the first book of the Psalter. It is a response to the appeal at the end of Psalm 32 to "be glad in the LORD, and rejoice, O righteous" (v. 11). Psalm 33 essentially praises God for his work in creation (vv. 8–9) and for his continuing providential care (vv. 18–19). But this has implications for peoples who plot in vain (2:1). Whereas their plans will be frustrated, God's will stands forever (33:10–11).

> The LORD brings the counsel of the nations to nothing;
>   he frustrates the plans of the peoples.
> The counsel of the LORD stands forever,
>   the plans of his heart to all generations.
> Blessed is the nation whose God is the LORD,
>   the people whom he has chosen as his heritage!
>   (Ps. 33:10–12)

Clearly the nations believe their armies will achieve their goals, but the psalmist affirms their ineffectiveness.

> The king is not saved by his great army;
>   a warrior is not delivered by his great strength.
> The war horse is a false hope for salvation,
>   and by its great might it cannot rescue. (vv. 16–17)

Only if God is on their side will the military succeed (vv. 18–19). Exactly what the nations were planning is left unsaid. But in the light of Psalm 2 and Psalms 46–48, an assault on Jerusalem seems the most likely plan. These psalms promise God's protection of the city, but like the promise of an eternal Davidic dynasty, this hope too seems to have been disproved by history in the era that the psalms were collected. Psalm 44 gives poignant voice to this feeling.

> But you have rejected us and disgraced us
>   and have not gone out with our armies.
> You have made us turn back from the foe,
>   and those who hate us have gotten spoil.
> You have made us like sheep for slaughter
>   and have scattered us among the nations.
> You have sold your people for a trifle,
>   demanding no high price for them.
> You have made us the taunt of our neighbors,
>   the derision and scorn of those around us.
> You have made us a byword among the nations,
>   a laughingstock among the peoples. (vv. 9–14)

This is the first psalm attributed to the sons of Korah and probably dates from pre-exilic times, perhaps the same time as Psalm 60, with which it has many affinities.[10] Some defeat by surrounding nations prompts this outburst. The psalm insists that the defeat cannot be attributed to some major sin (44:17), so why did God let it happen? He must have gone to sleep (v. 23)! In the postexilic period, when they made a strenuous effort to keep the law, the Jews must have asked the same question. The next group of psalms suggest some answers.

Psalm 45 may originally have been a royal wedding song. But in its present setting it is to be understood as a messianic psalm: the Messiah is marrying his bride, Israel. Verse 2 says,

> You are the most handsome of the sons of men;
>   grace is poured upon your lips;
>   therefore God has blessed you forever.

It is rendered by the Jewish Targum,

---

[10] Kirkpatrick, *The Book of Psalms*, 236.

Thy beauty, O King Messiah, exceeds that of the children
of men;
a spirit of prophecy is bestowed upon thy lips.

Verse 10, an address to the bride, "Hear, O daughter, and consider, and incline your ear," is translated, "Hear, O congregation of Israel, the law of his mouth, and consider his wondrous works."

The messianic interpretation is of course presupposed by the New Testament in such passages as Hebrews 1:8–9 and passages where the church is described as the bride of Christ, as well as those likening the kingdom of heaven to a wedding.

Whereas Psalm 44 bewailed Israel's oppression by her enemies, Psalm 45 looks forward to their submission to king Messiah: "The peoples fall under you" (v. 5); "The people of Tyre will seek your favor with gifts" (v. 12); and "nations will praise you forever and ever" (v. 17). Vesco sums up the relationship between the two psalms well.

> After the supplication of Psalm 44, which wondered about a possible rejection of Israel by Yahweh and presented the elect people as animals destined for the slaughter house, Psalm 45 brings a message of hope. It conjures up the messianic reign, it recalls the ancient promises, and it announces a glorious future for a people humiliated by a foreign occupier. The messiah, victorious priest and king, will reign with law and justice. His people will be married to him. Psalm 45 has led us to the temple of Jerusalem. And it is about Jerusalem that Psalm 46 is going to speak.[11]

Psalms 46–48 are often called Songs of Zion for they celebrate Jerusalem as the city where God dwells and which he protects. The nations may attack Jerusalem, but they will be thwarted because the Lord lives there. Psalm 46 says,

God is in the midst of her; she shall not be moved;
God will help her when morning dawns.

---

[11] Vesco, *Le psautier de David traduit et commenté*, 421 (my trans.).

The nations rage, the kingdoms totter;
　　he utters his voice, the earth melts.
The LORD of hosts is with us;
　　the God of Jacob is our fortress.　　*Selah*

Come, behold the works of the LORD,
　　how he has brought desolations on the earth.
He makes wars cease to the end of the earth;
　　he breaks the bow and shatters the spear;
　　he burns the chariots with fire.
"Be still, and know that I am God.
　　I will be exalted among the nations,
　　I will be exalted in the earth!" (vv. 5–10)

Psalm 47 continues in the same vein.

Clap your hands, all peoples!
　　Shout to God with loud songs of joy!
For the LORD, the Most High, is to be feared,
　　a great king over all the earth.
He subdued peoples under us,
　　and nations under our feet.
He chose our heritage for us,
　　the pride of Jacob whom he loves. (vv. 1–4)

Note now a new element. The peoples are summoned to clap their hands and shout for joy *because* they have been defeated (v. 3). This implies a fundamental change of attitude. They have been converted. They recognize the lordship of the God of Israel, and this makes them and their leaders part of the people of the God of Abraham.[12]

God reigns over the nations;
　　God sits on his holy throne.
The princes of the peoples gather

---

[12] The Hebrew of Ps. 47:9a is literally "the princes of the peoples have gathered, people of the God of Abraham." The second phrase, "people . . . Abraham" seems to be in apposition to "the princes of the peoples," hence the ESV inserts "as."

as the people of the God of Abraham.
For the shields of the earth belong to God;
    he is highly exalted! (vv. 8–9)

After this remarkable openness to the possibility that all the nations will join in the worship of the God of Israel, they reappear in the more typical guise in Psalm 48, attacking the city of God, where again they are defeated.

Within her citadels God
    has made himself known as a fortress.

For behold, the kings assembled;
    they came on together.
As soon as they saw it, they were astounded;
    they were in panic; they took to flight.
Trembling took hold of them there,
    anguish as of a woman in labor.
By the east wind you shattered
    the ships of Tarshish.
As we have heard, so have we seen
    in the city of the LORD of hosts,
in the city of our God,
    which God will establish forever. (vv. 3–8)

This oscillation between the nations' attacking the city of God, on the one hand, and acknowledging the sovereignty of the son of David and worshipping his God, on the other, characterizes the rest of the Psalter. The failure of their attacks, it is hoped, will lead to submission and worship, but that is obviously not always the case. Nevertheless, the attitude to the nations seems to become more positive as one reads on, in much the same way as laments become fewer and hymns of praise become more frequent later in the Psalter.

Three consecutive psalms (66–68) speak of the whole earth or all the nations or their kings praising the Lord or bringing him tribute. Psalm 66:4 declares,

> All the earth worships you
>> and sings praises to you.

Psalm 68:29 affirms,

> Because of your temple at Jerusalem
>> kings shall bear gifts to you.

And even more strikingly,

> Nobles shall come from Egypt;
>> Cush shall hasten to stretch out her hands to God. (v. 31)

Sandwiched between these two psalms comes Psalm 67, which repeatedly urges all the peoples and nations to praise God.

> May God be gracious to us and bless us
>> and make his face to shine upon us,   *Selah*
> that your way may be known on earth,
>> your saving power among all nations.
> Let the peoples praise you, O God;
>> let all the peoples praise you!
>
> Let the nations be glad and sing for joy,
>> for you judge the peoples with equity
>> and guide the nations upon earth.   *Selah*
> Let the peoples praise you, O God;
>> let all the peoples praise you!
>
> The earth has yielded its increase;
>> God, our God, shall bless us.
> God shall bless us;
>> let all the ends of the earth fear him! (vv. 1–7)

The same Hebrew tense is used through most of the psalm, and it may be translated as a jussive (let *x* happen) or as a future prediction (*x* will happen). In the opening verses the sense is clearly jussive, and in the last two verses, future. But what about verse 5?

Should it be translated, "Let the peoples praise you," jussive, as in most English translations, or with Kirkpatrick, "The peoples will praise you"?[13] The latter is a more satisfying climax and prepares the way for the predictions of Psalm 68:29, 31. Kirkpatrick explains: "The theme of this magnificent psalm is the march of God to victory. It traces the establishment of His kingdom in Israel in the past; it looks forward to the defeat of all opposition in the future, until all the kingdoms of the world own the God of Israel as their Lord and pay Him homage."[14]

The issue of jussive versus future surfaces again in Psalm 72. In this prayer for Solomon, it makes best sense to translate the verbs as jussives:

> May he have dominion from sea to sea . . . !
> May desert tribes bow down before him.
> > (72:8–9, ESV; similarly RSV, NRSV)

But if we read the passage messianically, a future sense is perhaps preferable: "He shall have dominion . . . . shall bow before him" (KJV; cf. NIV). Though one might pray for the new David to enjoy universal dominion, it would seem more consonant with other passages to see that dominion as promised. But whether we take Psalm 72 as hopes or promises, there is no doubt that the ultimate fulfillment involves all nations acknowledging the rule of the Messiah. As Psalm 86:9 puts it so clearly,

> All the nations you have made shall come
> > and worship before you, O Lord,
> > and shall glorify your name.

The next psalm develops these ideas in an amazing way.

> On the holy mount stands the city he founded;
> > the LORD loves the gates of Zion

---

[13] Kirkpatrick, *The Book of Psalms*, 374.
[14] Ibid., 375.

> more than all the dwelling places of Jacob.
> Glorious things of you are spoken,
>> O city of God. *Selah*
>
> Among those who know me I mention Rahab and Babylon;
>> behold, Philistia and Tyre, with Cush—
>> "This one was born there," they say.
> And of Zion it shall be said,
>> "This one and that one were born in her";
>> for the Most High himself will establish her.
> The LORD records as he registers the peoples,
>> "This one was born there." *Selah*
>
> Singers and dancers alike say,
>> "All my springs are in you." (Ps. 87:1–7)

Verses 4–6 are the words of God. He declares that Israel's traditional great enemies, Egypt (Rahab) and Babylon and the Philistines, are being granted citizenship of Jerusalem. The formula granting this citizenship is that "this one was born there." Other peoples mentioned, such as the Cushites from Nubia and the people of Tyre, show that the list is representative of all the peoples of the world. The names mentioned mark the four heavenly quarters: west (Egypt), east (Babylon), north (the land of the Philistines and Tyre), and south (Cush).[15]

In Psalm 45 Israel has been pictured as the bride of the Messiah. Here in Psalm 87 we have another picture: Jerusalem (its inhabitants) is the mother of the nations. They enjoy a relationship to God similar to Israel's, for God declares that they know him (v. 4). Kirkpatrick sums up the import of this psalm magnificently.

> This psalm is fittingly placed here, for it expands the thought of 86:9 in the style and the spirit of prophecy. It is terse, abrupt, enigmatic, like a prophetic oracle; in its breadth of view and fulness of Messianic hope it vies with the grandest of prophetic

---

[15] Frank-Lothar Hossfeld and Erich Zenger, *Psalms 2: A Commentary on Psalms 51–100*, trans. Linda M. Maloney (Minneapolis: Augsburg, 2005), 385.

utterances. It depicts Zion as the metropolis of the universal kingdom of God, into which all nations are adopted as citizens. The franchise of Zion is conferred upon them as though it were theirs by right of birth.

Thus the Psalm is a prediction of the incorporation of all nations into the Church of Christ, and the establishment of the new and universal nationality of the kingdom of God.[16]

Or to put it Zenger's way: "The world revolution of Psalm 2 becomes transformed into a great world family in Psalm 87, when Zion as the mother of messianic Israel (Psalm 2) and mother of all mankind (Psalm 87) becomes the capital of the world king Yahweh himself. That is the great theme of the fourth book of the Psalter."[17]

The last psalm of book 3 is Psalm 89, which is a prolonged lament over the end of the Davidic monarchy. In it the psalmist complains that God seems to have forgotten his promise to David.

> Of old you spoke in a vision to your godly one, and said: . . .
> "Once for all I have sworn by my holiness;
> > I will not lie to David.
> His offspring shall endure forever,
> > his throne as long as the sun before me. . . ."
>
> But now you have cast off and rejected;
> > You are full of wrath against your anointed. . . .
>
> Lord, where is your steadfast love of old,
> > which by your faithfulness you swore to David?
> > > (89:35–36, 38, 49)

It seems to many modern commentators that the next book of the Psalter (Psalms 90–106) answers this lament. At the heart of book 4 is a group of psalms celebrating the Lord's kingship. Mowinckel sees these psalms as used in the autumn festival of tabernacles when God was ritually enthroned as king. It is not necessary

---

[16] Kirkpatrick, *The Book of Psalms*, 518–19.
[17] Lohfink and Zenger, *Der Gott Israels und die Völker*, 150 (my trans.).

to adopt this theory to see that Psalms 93–100 do indeed focus on the Lord's reign; several of them begin with or include the cry, "The LORD reigns." Though some commentators see this reign of God as a substitute for a messianic king, this seems unlikely, given the prominence of the messianic psalms at key places in the Psalter. It is also unlikely because clearly royal/messianic psalms appear in the fifth and final book of the Psalter, for example, Psalms 110 and 132. But there is no doubt that the hope of the conversion of the Gentiles is reinforced in the fourth book. Consider Psalm 96:

> Oh sing to the LORD a new song;
> > sing to the LORD, all the earth!
> Sing to the LORD, bless his name;
> > tell of his salvation from day to day.
> Declare his glory among the nations,
> > his marvelous works among all the peoples! . . .
>
> Ascribe to the LORD, O families of the peoples,
> > ascribe to the LORD glory and strength!
> Ascribe to the LORD the glory due his name;
> > bring an offering, and come into his courts!
> Worship the LORD in the splendor of holiness;
> > tremble before him, all the earth!
>
> Say among the nations, "The LORD reigns!
> > Yes, the world is established; it shall never be moved;
> > he will judge the peoples with equity." (vv. 1–3, 7–10)

Note how verse 1 summons all the earth to sing to the Lord. That means that his saving deeds have to be proclaimed to all nations (v. 3). Then verse 8 urges the nations to come to the temple with their sacrifices, and verse 9 makes it clear that this applies to the whole earth. Verse 10 may even be the confession of the peoples worshipping the Lord in Jerusalem.[18] Whereas in verses 1–3 Israel proclaims God's deeds in history, here in verse 10 the nations

---

[18] Ibid., 161.

"confess YHWH, the king and sustainer of the world, with a quotation from 93:1."[19] Similar sentiments to those in Psalm 96 are found in Psalm 98.

> Oh sing to the LORD a new song,
>> for he has done marvelous things!
> His right hand and his holy arm
>> have worked salvation for him.
> The LORD has made known his salvation;
>> he has revealed his righteousness in the sight of the nations.
> He has remembered his steadfast love and faithfulness
>> to the house of Israel.
> All the ends of the earth have seen
>> the salvation of our God.
>
> Make a joyful noise to the LORD, all the earth;
>> break forth into joyous song and sing praises!
> Sing praises to the LORD with the lyre,
>> with the lyre and the sound of melody!
> With trumpets and the sound of the horn
>> make a joyful noise before the King, the LORD! (Ps. 98:1–6)

God's saving deeds prompt a new song (v. 1). The nations see it (v. 2), so all the earth must burst forth into joyful song (vv. 4–5).

But all these remarks are capped by Psalm 100, which Zenger declares is the most spectacular statement of theology in the Old Testament. Already we have been told that the nations will hear of God's deeds, confess that he is king, and offer sacrifices in Jerusalem. Now they appropriate the covenant formula to themselves. Like Israel, they see themselves in a covenant with the Lord. The nations say:

> Know that the LORD, he is God!
>> It is he who made us, and we are his;
>> we are his people, and the sheep of his pasture. (Ps. 100:3)

---

[19] Hossfeld and Zenger, *Psalms 2*, 466.

Zenger writes:

> If we read Psalms 93–100 as a continuing context, the nations move steadily into the center of the event, drawing closer and closer to Israel and its God.
>
> Psalm 100, as the climax of the composition, integrates the nations of the world in worship before the God of Zion: they should, and they will, shout aloud to YHWH, serve him (and not the idols; cf. 97:7) with joy, and experience his nearness—like Israel and together with it.[20]

Not all commentators share Zenger's daring reading that makes verse 3 a confession by the nations, but it is clear that this psalm calls on all of them to join in the true worship of the God of Israel.

In the fifth and final book of the Psalter, Psalms 107–50, we find the five themes set out in Psalm 2 reaffirmed. God's choice of David and his successors is reaffirmed in Psalm 132:11.

> The LORD swore to David a sure oath
>   from which he will not turn back;
> "One of the sons of your body
>   I will set on your throne."

Also reaffirmed is the election of Zion as God's dwelling place in several of the Songs of Ascents (e.g., Psalms 122, 125, 132).

The third theme of the attack on Jerusalem and the Davidic king is not forgotten either, as in the most poignant Psalm 137.

> By the waters of Babylon,
>   there we sat down and wept,
>   when we remembered Zion. . . .
>
> Remember, O LORD, against the Edomites
>   the day of Jerusalem,
> how they said, "Lay it bare, lay it bare,
>   down to its foundations!"

---

[20] Ibid., 497.

O daughter of Babylon, doomed to be destroyed,
 blessed shall he be who repays you
  with what you have done to us! (vv. 1, 7–8)

When the Psalter was compiled, the Jews had only seen a partial answer to their prayers in Cyrus's conquest of Babylon, and they still looked for the Lord's anointed to conquer their foes.
In Psalm 110 the Lord declares:

"Sit at my right hand
until I make your enemies your footstool. . . ."

The Lord is at your right hand;
 he will shatter kings on the day of his wrath.
He will execute judgment among the nations,
 filling them with corpses. (vv. 1, 5–6)

Psalm 118 is a thanksgiving uttered by the hoped-for king entering Jerusalem in triumph. And Psalm 144 is a prayer by David for deliverance

 from the hand of foreigners,
whose mouths speak lies
 and whose right hand is a right hand of falsehood. (vv. 7–8)

The next-to-last psalm pictures God's warriors celebrating his victory over the powers of evil, the nations that oppose God's rule.

Let the high praises of God be in their throats
 and two-edged swords in their hands,
to execute vengeance on the nations
 and punishments on the peoples,
to bind their kings with chains
 and their nobles with fetters of iron,
to execute on them the judgment written!
 This is honor for all his godly ones.
Praise the LORD! (Ps. 149:6–9)

But this is not the Psalter's last word on the nations. The Psalms still hope that nations and their leaders will, as a result of his people's vindication, join in God's praise.

Psalm 148 bids all mankind (including the nations) to join in praising him.

> Kings of the earth and all peoples,
>> princes and all rulers of the earth!
> Young men and maidens together,
>> old men and children!
>
> Let them praise the name of the LORD,
>> for his name alone is exalted;
>> his majesty is above earth and heaven. (vv. 11–13)

And now the Psalter's very last words are

> Let everything that has breath praise the LORD!
> Praise the LORD! (Ps. 150:6)

Works Cited

Commentaries

Alexander, Joseph A. *The Psalms Translated and Explained*. 1873. Reprint, Grand Rapids: Baker, 1975.

Allen, Leslie C. *Psalms 101–150*. Waco, TX: Word, 1983.

Briggs, Charles A. *A Critical and Exegetical Commentary on the Book of Psalms*. Vols. 1–2. Edinburgh: T&T Clark, 1906.

Calvin, John. *A Commentary on the Psalms of David*. Vols. 1–3. Oxford: Tegg, 1840.

Delitzsch, Franz. *Biblical Commentary on the Psalms*. Vols. 1–3. 1871. Reprint, Grand Rapids: Eerdmans, n.d.

Eaton, John H. *The Psalms*. London: T&T Clark, 2003.

Hossfeld, Frank-Lothar, and Erich Zenger. *Die Psalmen II: Psalm 51–100*. Herders Theologischer Kommentar zum Alten Testament. Freiburg: Herder, 2000.

———. *Die Psalmen III: Psalm 101–150*. Herders Theologischer Kommentar zum Alten Testament. Freiburg: Herder, 2008.

———. *Psalms 2: A Commentary on Psalms 51–100*. Translated by Linda M. Maloney. Minneapolis: Augsburg, 2005.

Kidner, Derek. *Psalms 1–72*. Leicester: Inter-Varsity, 1973.

———. *Psalms 73–150*. Leicester: Inter-Varsity, 1975.

Kirkpatrick, A. F. *The Book of Psalms*. Cambridge: Cambridge University Press, 1902.

Kraus, Hans-Joachim. *Psalmen 1–59*. Neukirchen: Neukirchener Verlag, 2003.

Motyer, J. Alec. "The Psalms." In *New Bible Commentary*, edited by Gordon J. Wenham, J. Alec Motyer, Donald A. Carson, and R. T. France, 485–583. Leicester: Inter-Varsity, 1994.

Seybold, Klaus. *Die Psalmen*. Tübingen: Mohr, 1996.

Vesco, Jean-Luc. *Le psautier de David traduit et commenté*. Paris: du Cerf, 2006.

Other Works

Alter, Robert. *The Art of Biblical Narrative*. New York: Basic Books, 1981.

———. *The Art of Biblical Poetry*. New York: Basic Books, 1985.

Athanasius, *On the Incarnation with appendix "On the Interpretation of the Psalms."* Edited and translated by a religious of C.S.M.V. New York: St Vladimir's Seminary Press, 1977.

Austin, J. L. *How to Do Things with Words*. Oxford: Oxford University Press, 1962.

Auwers, Jean-Marie. *La composition littéraire du psautier: Un état de la question*. Paris: Gabalda, 2000.

Bainton, Roland H. *Here I Stand: A Life of Martin Luther*. New York: Mentor, 1955.

Braulik, G. "Psalter and Messiah: Towards a Christological Understanding of the Psalms in the Old Testament and the Church Fathers." In *Psalms and Liturgy*, edited by D. J. Human and C. J. A. Vos, 15–40. London: T&T Clark, 2004.

Briggs, Richard S. *Words in Action: Speech Act Theory and Biblical Interpretation*. Edinburgh: T&T Clark, 2001.

Carr, David M. *Writing on the Tablet of the Heart*. New York: Oxford University Press, 2005.

Childs, Brevard S. *Introduction to the Old Testament as Scripture*. London: SCM, 1979.

Clements, Ronald E. "Worship and Ethics: A Re-examination of Psalm 15." In *Worship in the Hebrew Bible: Essays in Honor of John T. Willis*, edited by M. P. Graham, R. R. Marrs, and S. L. McKenzie, 78–94. Sheffield: Sheffield Academic Press, 1999.

Cole, R. L. *The Shape and Message of Book 3 (Psalms 73–89)*. Sheffield: Sheffield Academic Press, 2000.

Driver, S. R. *An Introduction to the Literature of the Old Testament*. Edinburgh: T&T Clark, 1894.

Eaton, John H. *Kingship in the Psalms.* London: SCM, 1976.

Evans, Donald D. *The Logic of Self-Involvement.* London: SCM, 1963.

Ford, David F., and Daniel W. Hardy. *Living in Praise: Worshipping and Knowing God.* London: Darton, Longman and Todd, 2005.

Goulder, Michael D. *The Prayers of David (Psalms 51–72).* Sheffield: JSOT Press, 1990.

Griffiths, Paul J. *Religious Reading: The Place of Reading in the Practice of Religion.* New York: Oxford University Press, 1999.

Gunkel, Hermann. *Die Psalmen.* Göttingen: Vandenhoeck & Ruprecht, 1926.

Holladay, William L. *The Psalms through Three Thousand Years.* Minneapolis: Fortress, 1993.

Houston, Walter J. "The King's Preferential Option for the Poor: Rhetoric, Ideology and Ethics in Psalm 72," *Biblical Interpretation* 7 (1999): 341–67.

Howard, David M. *The Structure of Psalms 93–100.* Winona Lake, IN: Eisenbrauns, 1997.

Jacob, Benno. "Die Reihenfolge der Psalmen." *Zeitschrift für die alttestamentliche Wissenschaft* 18 (1898): 99–119.

Johnston, Philip S., and David G. Firth, eds. *Interpreting the Psalms: Issues and Approaches.* Leicester: Apollos, 2005.

Kleer, Martin. *Der liebliche Sänger der Psalmen Israels.* Bodenheim: Philo, 1996.

Kraus, Hans-Joachim. *Geschichte der historisch-kritischen Erforschung des Alten Testaments von der Reformation bis zur Gegenwart.* Neukirchen: Erziehungsvereins, 1956.

———. *Theology of the Psalms.* Translated by Keith Crim. Minneapolis: Fortress, 1992.

Lewis, C. S. *Reflections on the Psalms.* London: Collins, 1961.

Lohfink, Norbert. *In the Shadow of Your Wings.* Translated by Linda M. Maloney. Collegeville, MN: Liturgical Press, 2003.

Lohfink, Norbert, and Erich Zenger, *Der Gott Israels und die Völker.* Stuttgart: Katholisches Bibelwerk Verlag, 1994.

Mason, Rex A. *The Books of Haggai, Zechariah and Malachi.* Cambridge: Cambridge University Press, 1977.

McCann, J. Clinton, Jr. "The Book of the Psalms." In *The New Interpreter's Bible.* Vol. 4, edited by Leander E. Keck et al., 641–1280. Nashville: Abingdon, 1996.

———, ed. *The Shape and Shaping of the Psalter.* Sheffield: Sheffield Academic Press, 2000.

———. *A Theological Introduction to the Book of Psalms.* Nashville: Abingdon Press, 1993.

Miller, P. D. "The Beginning of the Psalter." In *The Shape and Shaping of the Psalter,* edited by J. Clinton McCann Jr., 83–92. Sheffield: Sheffield Academic Press, 2000.

Mitchell, David C. *The Message of the Psalter: An Eschatological Programme in the Book of Psalms.* Sheffield: Sheffield Academic Press, 1997.

Mowinckel, Sigmund. *The Psalms in Israel's Worship.* One-volume ed. Translated by D. R. Ap-Thomas. Grand Rapids: Eerdmans, 2004.

Moyise, Steve, and Maarten J. Menken, eds. *The Psalms in the New Testament.* London: T&T Clark, 2004.

Nasuti, Harry. "The Sacramental Function of the Psalms in Contemporary Scholarship and Liturgical Practice." In *Psalms and Practice,* edited by Stephen B. Reid, 78–89. Collegeville, MN: Liturgical Press, 2001.

Otto, Eckart. *Theologische Ethik des Alten Testaments.* Stuttgart: Kohlhammer, 1994.

Ramsey, P. "Liturgy and Ethics." *Journal of Religious Ethics* 7, no. 2 (1979): 139–71.

Robertson, Edwin. *My Soul Finds Rest in God Alone.* Guildford: Eagle, 2001.

Rodd, Cyril S. *Glimpses of a Strange Land: Studies in Old Testament Ethics.* Edinburgh: T&T Clark, 2001.

Searle, J. R. *Expression and Meaning.* Cambridge: Cambridge University Press, 1979.

Sternberg, Meir. *The Poetics of Biblical Narrative.* Bloomington: Indiana University Press, 1985.

Thiselton, Anthony C. *New Horizons in Hermeneutics.* London: HarperCollins, 1992.

Wagner, Andreas. *Sprechakte und Sprechaktanalyse im Alten Testament.* Beihefte zur Zeitschrift für die alttestamentliche Wissenschaft 253. Berlin: de Gruyter, 1997.

Wenham, Gordon J. *Story as Torah.* Grand Rapids: Baker, 2004.

Wenham, John W. *The Enigma of Evil: Can We Believe in the Goodness of God?* Guildford: Eagle, 1994.

Whybray, R. Norman. *Reading the Psalms as a Book.* JSOTSup 222. Sheffield: Sheffield Academic Press, 1996.

Wilson, Gerald H. *The Editing of the Hebrew Psalter.* Chico, CA: Scholars Press, 1985.

Wright, Christopher J. H. *Old Testament Ethics for the People of God.* Leicester: Inter-Varsity, 2004.

Zenger, Erich. *A God of Vengeance? Understanding the Psalms of Divine Wrath.* Translated by Linda M. Maloney. Louisville: Westminster John Knox, 1996.

———. "Was wird anders bei kanonischer Psalmenauslegung?" In *Ein Gott*, edited by Friedrich V. Reiterer, 397–413. Würzburg: Echter Verlag, 1991.

General Index

adultery, 50, 69, 112–13, 149, 154
Alexander, Joseph, 20
arrangement, 43, 59–61, 78, 86, 90
Asaph, 21, 60, 72, 75, 77, 79, 86
Athanasius, 15–17, 39–40, 47, 84
Augustine, 20–21, 84, 99
Austin, J. L., 25, 27, 29–30
authorship, 60–61, 68–69, 86–87, 100
Auwers, Jean-Marie, 78

Bachl, Gottfried, 139–40
Basil, 59
behabitives, 29–30
benediction, 60–61
Bernard of Clairvaux, 23
biblical criticism, 85–86
Bitter, Gottfried, 143
Bonhoeffer, Dietrich, 37
Briggs, Charles, 147
Brueggemann, Walter, 63
Bucer, Martin, 16, 85
Buggle, Franz, 136
Bunyan, John, 103–4

Calvin, John, 19, 37, 40, 85, 130–32, 134
canonical reading, 14, 57–79, 90–101, 162
Carr, David, 18
children, 55, 107, 112, 157
Childs, Brevard, 59, 79, 90
Church of England, 40, 129, 158
commissives, 29–32

confession, 32–35, 50–52, 75, 143, 182, 184
contextualization, 147–48
coronation psalms, 58, 89, 91, 94, 163
covenant blessings, 159, 172
creation, 41, 141, 148
Cyprian, 20–21

dating, 74, 79, 83, 86, 89, 147, 174
Davidic collection, 69–75, 96–101, 153–59, 165–86
Davidic covenant, 61–68, 91–96, 149–50, 157, 164, 181
Dead Sea Scrolls, 15
Decalogue, 107–18
deism, 85
Delitzsch, Franz, 20, 59, 85
deliverance, 63–65, 171, 185
devotionals, 13, 57, 77–78
Driver, S. R., 86–88
Duffield, George, 103–4

early church, 15–16, 39, 46–48, 55
Eaton, John, 89, 147
Enlightenment, 85
ethics, 106–23
Eusebius, 59
Evans, Donald, 28–34
evil, 48, 51, 132, 139, 185

family, 23, 55, 112
final-form exegesis, 60, 68, 72, 90
Fletcher, Andrew, 13, 18
Ford, David, 17–18

forgiveness, 51, 154, 157
form criticism, 58, 76, 82, 86–90

Gentiles, 83–84, 172, 182–83
God
    authority of, 23
    character of, 107
    commitment to, 34–35
    imitation of, 121–23
    judgment of, 26, 49, 118–21,
        135–45, 168–69
    kingdom of, 135, 158, 175–76,
        179, 181
    sovereignty of, 94, 151
    steadfast love of, 151–59
    submission to, 177
    wrath of, 76
grace, 76, 124, 152
Greeks, 18
Griffiths, Paul, 21–23
Gunkel, Hermann, 15, 57, 88–89

Handel, George F., 18, 81–82
hasidim, 126
heaven, 39, 43, 46, 153, 175, 180
Hebrew Bible, 77–78
Herbert, George, 24
hesed, 123–26, 152–59
historical setting, 78–80
holiness, 32
Homer, 18
Hossfeld, Frank-Lothar, 20, 58–59,
    71–76, 78
hymns, 23–25, 40, 104–5

idolatry, 51, 109–10, 155
imprecatory psalms, 120, 129–45
incarnation, 24, 85
Israelites, 18–19, 148–49, 155,
    167–86

Jacob, Benno, 59
Jennens, Charles, 82

Jerome, 59
Jerusalem, 180, 183, 185
Jesus
    as Messiah, 52–54, 99–101
    as the new David, 170
    second coming of, 137
    use of Psalms, 38–39, 46, 51–52,
        90, 142
justice, 49, 97, 121, 135, 139–45
Justin Martyr, 84

Kendrick, Graham, 24, 103–4
Kidner, Derek, 133–34
kingship psalms, 119
Kirkpatrick, A. F., 131–33, 167,
    179–81
Kleer, Martin, 69–71, 96
Kraus, Hans-Joachim, 89–90

laments, 43–50, 119
law, 25–26, 42–43, 65–68, 106–8,
    116–18
literary context, 78–79
liturgy, 13–35
Liturgy of Hours, 135–36
Lohfink, Norbert, 136, 171–72
Lord's Prayer, 23
Luther, Martin, 16–17, 40, 76, 85

Marcellinus, 15–16, 39, 120n14
Marcionism, 135
Masoretic text, 73
Mays, J. L., 47–48, 63
McCann, J. Clinton, 63, 67, 93, 120,
    143–45
meditation, 13, 55
memorization, 14–15, 18, 20–23, 55
mercy, 50–51, 149–52
messianic psalms, 52–54, 66–68, 72,
    82–101, 157, 174–75, 182
Metz, Johannes, 141–42
Miller, P. D., 63–65, 96–97
Mitchell, David, 84, 164–65

Motyer, Alec, 134
Mowinckel, Sigmund, 15, 57, 88–89, 181
Murphy, R. E., 63

oaths, 14, 27, 35, 94–95
obedience, 65–68
Otto, Eckart, 105

penitential psalms, 50–52
poor, 113–14, 144–45
postexilic era, 66, 73–74, 77–78, 86, 111, 157, 163, 170
praise, 41–45
prayer, 37–55
pre-exilic era, 15, 57, 72, 111, 174
prophecy, 78, 96, 171–72

Qumran, 60

Ratzinger, Joseph, 138
recitation, 26–27
redemption, 131, 154
Reformed tradition, 17–18, 40
resurrection, 85, 99
righteousness, 63–64, 76, 90–91, 107, 115–23, 162
Rodd, Cyril S., 105
Roman Catholicism, 18
royal psalms, 52, 64–67, 78, 89, 91, 96, 99, 182

Sabbath, 111, 115
salvation, 41, 169, 171

Searle, J. R., 25–28
Septuagint, 75, 83
sin, 50–52, 76, 143, 156
skepticism, 86
Songs of Ascent, 58, 60, 62, 86, 184
sons of Korah, 58, 60, 72, 79, 85, 174
speech-act theory, 14, 23–35, 120n14
spiritual warfare, 105n
suffering, 47–50, 54–55, 135

Targum, 75, 83, 174–75
temple worship, 14–15, 64, 87–88
Ten Commandments, 107–15, 154–55
Thiselton, Anthony, 120n14
titles, 68–70, 86–87, 90–101
tongue, 114–15

Vesco, Jean-Luc, 162, 170, 175
vows, 27–28

Wagner, Andreas, 32–33
Wesley, Charles, 103
Whybray, R. N., 65–68
wicked, 63–64, 107, 115–18, 162
Wilson, Gerald, 58–65, 67, 78, 93
wisdom, 62–63, 66, 78
wisdom redaction, 66–67
worship, 29, 105, 143, 177
Wright, Christopher, 106–7

Zenger, Erich, 20, 49, 58, 71–75, 78, 119, 134–43, 181, 184

Scripture Index

Genesis
1:26–28	65
14	94
20:13	125
21:23	125

Exodus
2:3–5	109
20:7	109, 109n, 110
20:8	111
20:12	111
20:16	114
32–34	156
32:8	155
32:9–33:23	155
32:13	157
33	154
33:12–16	124
33:13	154
34	156
34:5–7	155
34:6–7	123
34:7–9	156
34:11	157
34:28	113

Deuteronomy
6:4	32
6:5	32
6:7	55
27:15–16	26
27:18	26

Joshua
1:8	106n5

1 Samuel
book of	98

2 Samuel
book of	98
6:17	88
7	67
7:2	88
11–12	74

1 Kings
12:1–15	150

1 Chronicles
15:15–16	14
16:8–22	14
16:8–36	14
16:23–24	14
16:35–36	14

2 Chronicles
24:22	132

Ezra
9:6–15	52

Nehemiah
1:5–11	52
8:1–10	25
9:16–37	52
12:31–43	15
13:15–22	111

Psalms
1	16, 53, 54, 55, 61, 62, 63, 64, 65, 66, 77, 90, 106, 107, 115–16
1–41	52, 61, 149, 162, 164, 165, 166
1:1	59n5, 122
1:1–3	116
1:2	19

198 *Scripture Index*

1:2–3	106n5	5:6	114, 119
1:4	135–36	5:7	29
1:5–6	97	5:9	114
1:6	64, 117, 119, 135–36	5:12	116
		6	50
2	16, 52, 53, 54, 58, 61, 62, 63, 64, 65, 66, 68, 72, 81, 82, 84, 85n14, 89, 90, 93, 94, 98, 99, 119, 162, 164, 165, 166, 168, 173, 181, 184	6:9–10	97, 119
		7	69, 96, 96n23, 167
		7:2	112
		7:3–5	98, 122
		7:6	167
		7:8	167
2–41	61	7:8–9	26, 97
2–100	73	7:9	116
2:1	173	7:9–10	122
2:1–2	81	7:10	97
2:1–3	163, 165	7:11	97
2:1–6	162–63	7:15–16	120
2:1–9	119	7:17	29, 65, 167
2:3	81	8	65, 110, 135
2:4	81	8:1	65, 110
2:6	165	8:1–4	135
2:6–8	91	8:3	65
2:7	53, 165	8:4	54
2:7–8	30	8:4–6	65
2:7–9	61	8:9	65, 110
2:8	28	9	84, 96, 167
2:8–9	94, 165	9–13	99
2:9	81, 136, 171	9:2	65
2:11	163, 168	9:3	168
2:11–12	165	9:3–4	168
2:12	59n5, 64, 165n4	9:3–8	167–68
3	16, 47, 54, 64, 68, 69, 84, 88, 96, 96n23, 99, 165	9:5	117, 168
		9:10	122
		9:16–17	117
3–7	96, 99, 117	10–14	96
3–41	60, 68, 72, 86	10:3	113–14
3:1	54	10:7	114
3:1–2	166	10:8	112
3:3	166	10:9	113–14
3:4	166	10:12–14	122
3:7	117, 119, 166	10:15	48
3:8	166	11	85, 88
4	16	11:7	121, 122
4:2	114	12	136
5	16, 47	12:2	114
5:4–6	122	12:5	114
		13	44, 54

13:1	47	24	64, 84, 106, 172,
13:1–4	44		173
13:5–6	44	24:3–4	109, 172
13:6	47	24:4	110
14	121	25	172
14:4	114	25–28	96
14:5	116, 122	25:14	172
15	64, 106	26:4	114
15:2–4	114–15	26:10	114
16–17	96	27:4	85
17	47	27:12	115
17:12	112	28	47
18	64, 69, 89, 96,	28:3	115
	96n23, 168, 169,	30	42, 96
	170	30:1–2	42
18:7–15	67	30:4	126
18:20–24	66	30:4–5	42
18:25	126, 169	31	96
18:27	169	31:5	38
18:40	168–69	31:6	110
18:43–49	168–69	31:23–24	126
18:49	169	32	16, 50, 96
18:50	170	32:11	173
19	42, 64, 107	33	16, 173
19:1–6	66	33:8–9	173
19:7	42	33:10–11	173
19:7–14	66	33:10–12	173
20	64, 89, 96	33:16–17	173
21	64, 89	33:18–19	173
21:1	83	34	69, 96, 96n23
22	44, 45, 46, 54, 84,	34:3–5	31
	89, 90, 96, 99, 100,	34:13	115
	142, 172	34:15	116
22:1	38	34:17	116
22:1–20	170	34:21	117
22:12	112	35–36	96
22:13	112	35–41	75
22:16	112	35:11	115
22:18	114	35:17	112
22:21	170	35:20	115
22:24	170	36:1	157
22:27–28	170–71	37	63, 111n
22:27–30	87	37:14	118
22:30–31	171	37:17	116
23	135, 171, 172	37:21	118
23:5	135	37:28	126
		37:29	116

37:32	112, 118	50:23	75
37:35–36	118	51	16, 50, 69, 73, 74,
37:39	116		75, 76, 77, 96,
38	50, 111n		96n23, 113
38–39	96	51–65	60
38–41	59n7	51–72	70, 72, 74, 75
38:9	28	51–100	58
39:1	27	51:1	50, 75, 113
40–41	96	51:1–12	73
40:1–3	31	51:1–17	73, 74
40:8	64	51:4	75
41	16	51:5	76
41:1	59n5	51:12	75
41:11–12	61	51:13	51
41:13	61, 70, 72	51:14	75
42	18, 63	51:14–19	75
42–49	72	51:18	75
42–72	52, 61, 149	51:18–19	73, 74, 87
44	136, 175	52	69, 96, 96n23
44:9–14	174	52–68	72
44:17	174	52:2–5	115
44:20	110	54	69, 96, 96n23
44:23	174	54:3	112
45	15, 52, 89, 174,	55:3	118
	175, 180	56	15, 69, 96n23
45:2	174	56–57	96
45:5	175	56:9	69
45:10	175	56:9–11	115
45:12	175	56:21	115
45:17	175	57	69, 96n23
46	57, 175	58	136
46–48	173, 175	59	69, 96
46:5–10	175–76	59:12	115
47	84	60	69, 96n23, 174
47:1–4	176	63	69, 96, 96n23
47:3	176	64:2	118
47:8–9	176–77	64:3–5	115
47:9a	176n	65:2	73
48:3–8	177	65–68	73
50	72, 75, 84, 113	66–68	177
50:5	126	66:4	177–78
50:6	75	66:13–14	115
50:8–15	75	67:1–7	178
50:16	118	67:5	178
50:16–19	112–13	68	84
50:18	113	68–70	60
50:19–20	115	68:2	117

68:8	107	81	108, 108n
68:17	107	81:3	111
68:29	178, 179	81:9	109, 110
68:31	178, 179	81:10	108
69	15, 45, 73, 84, 89, 133	82	84, 144
		83	92, 136
69–71	59n7	86	47, 59n7, 155
69:1	27	86:2	126
69:1–2	45	86:8	109
69:4	45, 114, 115	86:9	179, 180
69:9	46	86:10	109
69:22–23	46	86:15	155n
69:25	46	87	180, 181
70:2	112	87:1–7	179–80
72	18, 52, 53, 54, 63, 66, 67, 70, 83, 84, 89, 91, 93, 98, 99, 106, 179	87:4	180
		87:4–6	180
		88	47, 59n7, 84, 92
		88:1–3	45
72:1–2	121	88:16–18	45
72:3	73	89	52, 53, 63, 66, 70, 72, 89, 92, 93, 94, 181
72:4	121		
72:5	67		
72:7	73	89:3–4	94
72:8	52, 82–83, 164	89:4	53
72:8–9	179	89:5	67
72:8–11	91, 149	89:15	59n5
72:11	52, 98	89:19–37	61
72:12	52	89:22	67
72:12–14	150	89:26	112
72:17	59n5, 61	89:28	157
72:18–19	61, 72	89:29	67
72:20	91	89:30	67
73	63, 66	89:35	94
73–83	72, 75, 86	89:35–36	164, 181
73–89	52, 53, 61	89:35–37	92
73:3–12	117–18	89:38	181
73:8–9	115	89:38–39	92
73:18–19	117–18	89:38–45	53
73:27	112n	89:38–49	151
74:2–3	92	89:39	62
75	16	89:41–42	92
75:4	118	89:46	53, 67
78	107, 108	89:49	62, 67, 92, 94, 181
78:5–8	108	89:52	61, 72
79	92	90	63, 66
79:10	46	90–92	72
80	15	90–106	52, 53, 62, 151, 181

90:1	62	102–3	71
90:1–4	151	103	14n, 18, 93, 123,
91:14	30		147, 148, 149, 157,
92	15, 111		158, 159
92:5–9	66	103:1	153
92:12–14	66	103:1–5	152
93	93	103:2	154
93–99	151	103:2–4	123
93–100	58, 73, 119, 182,	103:3–5	154
	184	103:4	152
93:1	62, 183	103:6–10	152, 154
94:3	46	103:7	154
94:6	112	103:7–12	124
95	93	103:8	152, 155
95:3	32, 93, 109	103:9	156
95:7	111	103:10	152
96	183	103:11	152, 156–57
96:1	182	103:11–12	156
96:1–3	182	103:11–14	152
96:1–13	14	103:13	156–57
96:3	182	103:14	153, 157
96:4	109	103:15	157
96:7–10	182	103:15–18	152
96:8	111, 182	103:17	151, 152, 156–57
96:9	182	103:18	158
96:10	62, 93, 182	103:19	151, 158
96:11–13	119	103:19–22	152
97:1	32, 62	103:20–22	158
97:3	184	104	33, 41, 148
97:7	110, 184	104–6	149
97:9	109	104:1–2	33, 41
98	183	104:3–30	33
98:1	183	104:5	41
98:1–6	183	104:24	33, 41
98:2	183	104:33–35	33
98:4–5	183	104–6	19, 77, 148
99:1	32, 62	105	41, 108, 148
99:3	111	105–6	93
100	15, 183, 184	105–7	107
100:1	161	105:1–15	14
100:3	183	105:44–45	108
101	71, 89, 121, 169	106	41, 93, 148
101–4	71	106:3	59n5
101:5	115	106:19	107
101:6–8	121–22	106:36	110
101:8	117	106:39	112n
102	50, 59n7, 71	106:40–41	148–49

106:44–46	149
106:47	93, 149
106:47–48	14
106:48	61
107	63, 66, 123
107–50	53, 184
107:8	123
107:15	123
107:21	123
107:31	123
108–9	71
108–10	62, 71, 94
109	130, 133, 136, 144, 145
109:2	115
109:6–19	144
109:12	125
109:16	125
109:31	145
110	52, 53, 58, 67, 71, 84, 88, 89, 94, 98, 182
110:1	98, 185
110:2	94
110:4	94
110:5–6	185
111–12	59n6
111:10	157
112	16
112:1	116, 117, 157
112:4–9	116–17
112:5	117
112:6	116
112:7–8	117
112:9	117
113–18	15n3, 38
113:7–9	121
114	107
115	41, 110
115–18	38
115:2–8	110
116	16
116:1	34
116:5	121
116:18–19	34
118	15, 34, 38, 185
118:5–6	38
118:17	38
118:19	38
118:22	38
118:24	111
118:25–26	15
119	16, 42, 59n6, 106, 107
119:12	106
119:26	106
119:29	106
119:33	106
119:64	106
119:66	106
119:68	106
119:84	46
119:97	22, 43
119:108	106
119:124	106
119:135	106
119:171	106
120–34	60, 62, 86
120:2–3	115
122	184
125	184
127:3	112
128	16
130	50
132	52, 53, 62, 67, 89, 94, 98, 182, 184
132:11	184
132:11–12	95, 164
132:14	95
132:17	95
134	16
135	110
135:15–18	110
136	41, 123
136:1–9	123
136:10–13	123
136:17–22	123
137	136, 143, 144, 184
137:1	184–85
137:4	71
137:7–8	184–85
138	84
138–45	59n6, 60, 62, 71, 94
138:4	71

139	121, 134, 136
139:21–22	130
140	47
140–43	59n7
140:3	115
142	69, 96, 96n23
143	50
144	52, 53, 63, 89
144:7–8	185
144:11	115
144:15	59n5
145	59n6, 63, 95, 155
145:1	95
145:8	155n
145:13	95
145:17	126
145:20	135
145:21	71
146–50	61, 71
146:9	117
147:6	117
148:11–13	186
149:5	126
149:6–9	171, 185
149:7	136
150	43, 63
150:6	186

Proverbs

3:3	125
16:6	125

Isaiah

1:13	111
2:2–4	171–72
31:4	19n14
38:14	19n14
53	99

Hosea

11:1	100

Joel

2:13	155n

Amos

8:5	111

Jonah

4:2	155n

Micah

4:1–5	171–72
7:18–20	156

Zechariah

9:10	82, 83
14:16–19	171–72

Matthew

2:14–15	100
5–7	21
6:10	48
22:41–46	84
26:30	38

Mark

11:9	15
12:35–37	84n4

Luke

15	75
15:18	75
15:21	75
18:13	75
20:41–44	84n4
23:46	38
24:25–26	54
24:26–27	99

John

2:17	46
15:25	45

Acts

1:20	46
7:60	132

Romans

1:18–3:31	76
3:4	75
10:9–10	34
11:9	46
15:3	46

1 Corinthians

12:26	145
13:4	25, 104n

14:26 15

Galatians
6:2 145

Ephesians
5:18 55
5:18–19 38
5:19 15

Colossians
3:16 15, 38, 55

Hebrews
1:8–9 175

James
3:9–10 115

1 Peter
4:13 54

1 John
1:9 51

Revelation
6:9–10 46